Recovering the African Feminine Divine in Literature, the Arts, and Practice

The Black Atlantic Cultural Series: Revisioning the Literary, Visual, and Performing Arts

Series Editor: Emily Allen-Williams, the
University of the Virgin Islands

This series will embrace exploratory discussions that emanate from the latest Africana ideas from the Caribbean, Black Atlantic, and Southern United States. The series aims to examine ideologies, theories, aesthetics, and their cultural and global manifestations. From the music, dance, literature, fashion, linguistic nuances, and beyond, Africana culture is vibrantly original and requires significant documentation to avoid its loss in the vast imitation that abounds nationally and internationally.

Recent titles in the series:
Art and Ritual in the Black Diaspora: Archetypes of Transition, by Paul A. Griffith
Recovering the African Feminine Divine in Literature, the Arts, and Practice: Yemonja Awakening, edited by LaJuan Simpson-Wilkey, Sheila Smith McKoy, and Eric Bridges

Recovering the African Feminine Divine in Literature, the Arts, and Practice

Yemonja Awakening

Edited by
LaJuan Simpson-Wilkey
Sheila Smith McKoy
Eric M. Bridges

LEXINGTON BOOKS
Lanham • Boulder • New York • London

Published by Lexington Books
An imprint of The Rowman & Littlefield Publishing Group, Inc.
4501 Forbes Boulevard, Suite 200, Lanham, Maryland 20706
www.rowman.com

6 Tinworth Street, London SE11 5AL, United Kingdom

British Library Cataloguing in Publication Information Available

Library of Congress Control Number: 2020945888

ISBN 978-1-7936-4093-2 (cloth)
ISBN 978-1-7936-4095-6 (pbk)
ISBN 978-1-7936-4094-9 (electronic)

Contents

Introduction

Ifakayode Faniyi Olayiwola, Eric Bridges,
Sheila Smith McKoy, and LaJuan Simpson-Wilkey

It is a great honor to pay homage to the most senior of all river deities. This collection of essays allows the world to see how subtle, yet vast, Yemonja's purvey is in human affairs. While many people see Yemonja as a maternal figure, we would be remiss if we do not appreciate her contributions as a goddess of arts and healing. Yemonja Awakening bridges aspects of the essence of her being an orisa who governs arts, healing, and transformation from the origin of her worship in Yorùbáland to the Americas and throughout the world.

This edited volume provides a context through which to understand the myriad ways in which the African feminine divine is being reclaimed by scholars, practitioners and cultural scholars worldwide. This volume also seeks to address the complex ways in which the reclamation of and recognition of Yemonja facilitates cultural survival and the formation of African-centric identity. In particular, these cultural practices are symbolically represented by Yemonja, the African female deity who is the mother of the entire world of the Orisa. As mother of the sphere of goddesses/gods, humans, plants, and animals, she is Omi Jori, leader of waters. This connotes her status and power over all realms of existence. Yemonja is the deity whose province is the Ogun River; however, in her power and desire to protect her children during the Middle Passage she became yemaya and Iemanya in the Americas. Since Yemonja also references sexual, creative, spatial, and spiritual energies, the editors and contributors see her as being pivotal to this project as an expansive and original cartography of impact of the African feminine divine globally. This work provides the context for understanding how the spiritual conceptualizations of the African feminine divine underpin critical cultural forms, even when it has been previously unacknowledged and despite the cultural encounters with European and Western models of being. This project explores the wide range of original and syncretic practices that reclaim the African feminine divine. As such, this collection captures the presence and essential characteristics of African spiritual practice and epistemologies in literature, film, contemporary public conversations, and cultural practices. This collection provides the necessary space in which critical scholarship, practitioner observations and applications, as well as artistry and activists focused on reclaiming the African feminine divine engage in the "bridge language" that Toni Cade Bambara calls for in her novel. As such, this anthology will occupy a unique space as a text engaging in scholarship, artistry, and practice focused on the impact of the African feminine divine in Africa and her global diaspora. This anthology will appeal widely to humanities and social science scholars, counselors and life coaches focused on African cultural practitioners, and adherents of Ifa.

Yemonja Awakening provides the context for understanding how the spiritual conceptualizations of the African feminine divine as exemplified by Yemonja underpin critical cultural forms, even when it has been previously unacknowledged and despite the cultural encounters with European and Western models of being. This project explores the wide range of original and syncretic practices, as demonstrated by the myriad of worship forms seen throughout the Americas, that reclaim the African feminine divine. As such, this collection captures the presence and essential characteristics of African spiritual practice and epistemologies in literature, film, contemporary public conversations and cultural and spiritual practices. This collection provides the necessary space in which critical scholarship, practitioner observations and applications, and artistry and activists focused on reclaiming the African feminine divine engage in the "bridge language" that Toni Cade Bambara calls for in her novel. As such, this anthology will occupy a unique space as a text engaging in scholarship, artistry, and practice focused on the impact of the African feminine divine in Africa and the global diaspora.

Yemonja is a major orisa of the Yoruba people of southwestern Nigeria. While this great goddess calls her original home Yorùbáland, her worship has spread throughout the world. She was carried by kidnapped West Africans across the Atlantic Ocean when they were enslaved and brought to the Americas, especially to the countries that became Cuba and Brazil, where she is considered the patron guardian of this nation. Yemonja is an orisa who inspires awe and reverence among believers worldwide. She is worshiped in such diverse nations including Mexico, Trinidad and Tobago, United States, Puerto Rico, Japan, Germany, Great Britain, and throughout Central America. Considering that she is an orisa of transformative power as seen through her depiction as a mermaid, she is ever becoming, and her essence is infinitely itself because she is so vast that she cannot be contained. Only Olokun, the Owner of Ocean, can truly absorb and integrate her energy. It is this transformative power that she bequeathed to her children who survived the Maafa. Indeed, Yemonja is an orisa who exemplifies evolution.

Yemonja also has a sacred relationship with the Yoruba people. She is the mother of many of the other orisa; including Sango, the owner of thunder, lighting, and rain as shown through her oriki or praise name, Iya Sango, Mother of Sango. Sango himself, being the magnificent warrior king, is so vast and ferocious that even the most powerful beings fear his might. Known as the Wrath of Olodumare, Sango's powers are to be respected and honored. However, being the adoptive son of Yemonja, it is only she who is powerful enough to carry Sango on her back. This is testament of Yemonja's strength physically as well as socially, for it is she as a mother supreme who can make kings. While Yemonja is a force of nature, she is also a political force who does not operate behind rulers, but creates them, and can remove them when their rulership no longer serves civilizations. On an esoteric level, this imagery of Yemonja carrying Sango on her back is symbolic of immortality in the form of Yemonja carrying mortality in the form of Sango, meaning that life and creation are eternal processes.

Yemonja is also mother and at times the wife of Ogun, the orisa of war, iron, civilization, poets, and agriculture. Again, we see her influence in civilization creation and maintenance through her relationship with Ogun. She is said to have raised the son of the ancient and mysterious orisa, Nana Buruku, Obaluaiye, the Great Lord of the Earth, disease and healing. As of this writing, humanity finds itself under the scourge of Covid-19 and our appeals to the Lord of the Earth are crucial to the survival of humanity. However, Obaluaiye gets his power of healing from his adoptive mother, Yemonja, who is a healer in the truest sense of the word. Being a supreme mother, all of creation can call out to her for physical, psychological, or spiritual healing. At this time, the world is in need of her power to heal us as a global civilization. May Yemonja Awoyo hear our pleas and allow us to transform to something better, more magical, and majestical than we are now.

Note: Ifakayode Faniyi Olayiwola is the Agbongbon of Osogboland Osun State Nigeria.

Part I

YEMONJA

DEFINITIONS AND PRACTICE

Chapter 1

The Opulent Mother

Brief Discussion of Yemonja and Her Worship in Yorùbáland

Eric M. Bridges

As a priest of Yemonja my familiarity with Yemonja came early in my life even though I was not aware of who she was. As a child I would have dreams of this goddess who would rise from mystical waters and walk with me and guide me throughout my life. I was born into a family that was African Methodist Episcopalian and raised Baptist in the southeastern United States. I had no religious reference to Yemonja or any of the other òrìsà that I would also dream about during my childhood. As fantastical as this sounds (I am a psychologist and for years would not have ever told anyone of my dreams) I knew that this goddess was a real entity. Over the course of my life I would read about various African goddesses and gods. It was not until I finished graduate school and began teaching psychology at an American university that I was "officially" introduced to Yemonja. In a class that I teach called the Psychology of the African American Experience, I became acquainted with Tjade "Osuntinibu" Wright. Tjade Wright is an Osun priestess initiated through the òrìsà/vodun system of Oyotunjí Village of Sheldon, South Carolina. One evening after the semester ended she agreed to meet with me to discuss Yemonja. She suggested that I receive a divination from a priest of Ifá, a babaláwo. This divination changed my life. After this divination I embraced òrìsà worship, subsequently being initiated to the priesthoods of Yemonja and Ifá.

Òrìsà worship is a global phenomenon. According to Kólá Abímbólá there are over 100 million practitioners of òrìsà worship worldwide. This includes traditional West African Orísá worship (also known as Isese, meaning "origin"), Candomblé (Brazil), Santeria (Cuba), Ochá de Reglá (Puerto Rico), and the Òrìsà Vodun system of Oyotunjí Village. Depending on the aforementioned traditions, Yemonja is conceived differently. Among West African Orísá worshippers (Isese), Yemonja is the òrìsà of the Ogun River in Nigeria. Yemonja, the gatekeeper of the wilderness in that main tributary have their origins in the wilderness (Freeman, 2019). Among New World practitioners of òrìsà worship, Yemaya, who Yemonja becomes in the New World, is the guardian of the top layer of the ocean, while Olokun (owner of the ocean) is the òrìsà who governs the bottom half of the ocean.

The belief that Yemaya is the ruler of the top layer of the ocean, particularly the Atlantic Ocean, is rooted in the Maafa, also known as the Transatlantic Slave Trade, where millions of Africans were kidnapped, enslaved, and brought to the many countries throughout the Western Hemisphere. Many Africans who were kidnapped and enslaved by European colonizers were Yorùbá people who were brought in vast numbers to Brazil and Cuba. On the ships that held their bodies on which they experienced torture, rape, starvation, and loneliness, they believed that Yemaya was there with them. Even though this passage was the most hellish experience in human history, the enslaved Yorùbá people believed that Yemonja, who became Yemaya in the New World, was with them as a mother protecting her children. While many New World òrìsà worshippers see Yemaya as the protector of the top layer of the ocean, Isese traditionalists view Yemonja as the guardian of the Ogun River. What all worshippers globally agree on is Yemonja being a paramount maternal òrìsà along with Osun, Oya, Odù, Obba, Nana Buruku, Korikotó, Yewá, and many other feminine òrìsà in the Yorùbá pantheon. The focal point of this chapter will be a brief analysis of Yemonja worship in Nigeria.

ESTABLISHING RAPPORT WITH ÒRÌSÀ

The worship of an òrìsà is personal to practitioners of òrìsà worship. Òrìsà worship has both formal ways of approaching the òrìsà as well as less formal ways of approaching òrìsà. There are certain body positions that must be adhered to when making supplication (appeasement) to the òrìsà. According to Ifakayode Faniyi Olayiwole, the Agbongbon (chief Ifa priest) of Osogboland in Osun State, when praying to or making appeasement to òrìsà such as Yemonja, Obàtálá, Osun, Olokun, and Ifá practitioners kneel to pay respect. When appeasing or praying to Èsù, Ògún, and Egúngún (a family's elevated ancestors) one must stand when paying respect to these powerful entities. When worshipping the òrìsà of thunder and lighting, Sàngö, the supplicant squats while praying or making appeasement.

Hand gestures can also be used to evoke the òrìsà. According to Nathan Lugo, a babaláwo priest of Obàtálá and Egúngún, a person can hold their hands out while praying or gently rub them together. While these are formalized and necessary positions that must be followed to demonstrate respect for the òrìsà, worshippers can establish less formal relationships with the deities in order to fully connect with them. A practitioner of òrìsà worship may simply talk with the òrìsà in an informal fashion in order to connect fully with them. These simple acts are demonstrative of the fact òrìsà worship is not a religion, but a way of life, a culture. While Yorùbá spirituality encompasses the worship of the many 400+1 òrìsà, the most important òrìsà that an individual can worship is Iwá Pelé (good or gentle character) and Òrì Ìnù, a person's inner divinity. Regarding Iwá Pelé, gentle or good character is not synonymous with meekness or a "turn the other cheek" mentality. Character is determined by how one chooses to evolve in response to the many challenges that humans experience. For example, if a person is being attacked on a physical, psychological, or spiritual level it is good character to defend oneself. This also applies to collective groups of people. If a person or group of people are being attacked and they do not attempt to stop the attack by defending themselves, they are displaying bad character. The òrìsà therefore become templates for human behavior. Sometimes it may be best to deal with a particular situation diplomatically, like Yemonja, Obàtátá, Ifá, or Osun. There are times that it is best to handle conflictual circumstances in a war-like manner, like the òrìsà Oya, Sàngö, and Ogún. While these deities are known for their warlike disposition, they also have a gentle nature. However, it must be stated that while the formerly mentioned órìsà tend to be "cool," they also have a warrior's disposition when offended egregiously. Lastly, while Yorùbá is a cosmopolitan and intellectual culture, it is also a warrior culture. The òrìsà are reflective of these cultural characteristics of the Yorùbá people.

Yemonja in Yorùbáland

Yemonja primarily is known as a nurturing órìsá. As a mother supreme, she has many children, all species on planet earth may call her mother. Thus, her full name, Iye Omo Eja roughly translates as "mother of fishes" or "mother whose children are numerous as fishes" is an allusion to her role as a generative force in creation, as well as a divinity of multiplicity and infinity. Yemonja is an òrìsà who is commensurate with life itself. Indeed, her children are so varied and diverse that they are essentially uncountable; from the smallest amoeba to òrìsà. According to stories from various areas in Yorùbáland, it was Yemonja who gave the water of life to Obàtálá in the creation of humankind. Given that Orisanla (Obàlátá) is a Funfun deity (white, not to be confused with skin color but as a primordial òrìsà of light) and his association with the color white, Yemonja's color in West African òrìsà worship is also white. In Isese tradition, the sacred gourd that holds her stones and other emblems is painted with efun, a white chalk like substance in honor of her relationship with the first among equals among the òrìsà, Obàtálá. Also, in Isese worship, priestesses and priests of Yemonja wear white in keeping with this understanding that Yemonja and Obàbátá are co-creative forces, dependent on one another for the survival of life on earth. However, while Yemonja is a nurturing energy, readily available to create and sustain life, she has a destructive aspect that, while she does not express often, when she is angered, the effects of her anger will be catastrophic. In the event that she is aroused or becomes "heated" her priesthood wears the color pink to "cool" her down in some Yoruba towns (Freeman, 2019). This attribute she shares with the most senior of all water òrìsà, Olokun, the owner of the ocean.

In various towns in Nigeria Yemonja's priests have a taboo against eating eja abori (catfish); however, in the city of Abeokuta it is not taboo for priests to eat it, but it is taboo for them to sell catfish (Freeman, 2019). As a major maternal òrìsà Yemonja is highly associated with the birthing of children and is known to provide mothers with many children. In some Odu Ifá ese (poetic verses) Yemonja is spoken of as having many children, though she would not become a mother until the later part of her life in her many manifestations.

An òrìkì of Yemonja that shows the prominence of Yemonja to the Yorùbà is Okere Okun, the senior river deity who goes directly to the sea without paying homage to any other river deities. Analogous to her status as mother to the òrìsà, she is literally the mother river in Yorùbáland in that all other river deities must pay homage to her. Yemonja is also known as Apota Pele Pe, the One who Kills the Enemy and Makes the Curse Potent as well as Jogun Oso, the One Who Inherits the Curse. These last two original are important allusions to Yemonja's relationship with the Oso, the male ajé. The spelling of her name as Yemonja in this chapter and the volume itself is reflective of this as well. Iye Omo Ni Eja, roughly translates as the Mother Whose Children are as Numerous as Fishes Who Is Connected to the Wizards. The word, Ni speaks of this mysterious connection that she has with the Oso (Freeman, 2019). Other òrìkì that describe Yemonja are Iyamogba (the mother who is associated with arts and crafts, especially pottery and dye). If one would see a traditional Yemonja shrine in Nigeria, they would see that her shrine is surrounded by carvings of nursing mothers with long breasts that represent her power as a deity of fecundity. As the spiritual mother of Sangó, she is called Iya Sàngò. Lastly, several other òrìkì that are used in order to summon Yemonja are Arugbo Odo (the elder of all the river deities) and Omi Jori (the leader of the river deities). In reverence to her primacy as the first of river òrìsà we hail Yemonja with, Omi ooo, water itself.

One of the Odu Ifà where Yemonja speaks prominently is Iwori Meji, the third of the sixteen major Odu Ifá. One ese or poem which provides a narrative of Yemonja was told to me by my oluwo or spiritual teacher, Ifakayode Faniyi Olayiwola:

Iwori Meji lo siketa Odu wa sile Aye
Adifa Fun Yemoja Awoyo
Ti mese lodo ti sigidi legbodo
Nti ikile Orun bo wa si taye
Nijoti Awoyo re Odo lo ko Omo were
Were, wa sile Aye

Iwori Meji
Divination was done for Yemonja Awoyo
The one that lives inside the river
Sigidi legbodo (another oriki or alias for Yemonja)
She was asked to perform ebo when she was coming from heaven to the earth
When Awoyo (oriki for Yemonja) stayed in the river is
    when many children came to the house.

In this verse of Iwori Meji we see that even the òrìsà get divination to aid in their evolution. Even Olodumare—the supreme being who receives Ifà divination, demonstrating that all of creation, humans, animals, plants, òrìsà—is constantly evolving and is striving to become more. A brief note on Olodumare regarding the belief that the Yorùbá supreme deity is the counterpart to the Abrahamic supreme deities of "God," Jehovah, or Allah. Olodumare is not synonymous with these later deities. Olodumare is a force that is everything in creation, the positive, neutral, and negative forces of creation. Olodumare is creation and destruction, beyond gender, and beyond explanation. In the ese from Iwori Meji we see Yemonja being the òrìsà who brings children to the earth. Children are most sacred in Yorùbá culture. Through children, continuation of the family lineage is continued, allowing us to see eternity. Therefore, Yemonja herself becomes an òrìsà of infinity and eternity.

In Nigeria, two food items especially sacred to Yemonja are greens and onions. A well-known Orin Yemonja (Yemonja song) in Yorùbáland that describes Yemonja's love of green and onions is as follows:

Yemonja, ooo
Yemonja, Hail
Yemonja, yé yé
Yemonja, Mother
Yemonja gbà
Yemonja, Accept this offering

Yemonja yé yé
Yemonja, Mother
Yemonja gbá
Yemonja, Accept this offering
Yemonja gbà'lùbosá ko fi r'òfó
Yemonja, take these onions as you prepare your green vegetables and soup
Yemonja yé yé
Yemonja, Mother

This orin (song) demonstrates Yemonja's power as a healer. Being an òrìsà of medicine Yemonja knows the secrets of plant medicine in order to heal her children. This song also subtly reminds us of her role as Jogun Oso, the one who fights off curses, which is one of the major Ajogun or warriors against mankind. Sickness and disease are Ajoguns, and Yemonja is a òrìsà who worshippers placate and appease to avoid these forces of destruction.

Other food items sacred to Yemonja include white corn porridge, asaro, red palm oil, salt, pounded yam, guinea hen, hippopotamus, and gin. Given Yemonja's status as an òrìsà of wealth, cowrie shells are also used to curry favor from her. In Nigeria, the metal that is associated to Yemonja is iron. Iron is a strong and durable metal: very much synonymous with the attributes of a strong mother who while nurturing, is also a warrior who is always prepared to defend her children. She shares this affinity with Ogun, who is one of her spiritual husbands along with Olufon (another funfun deity), and Òrìsà Oko who is an agriculture deity. In Isese worship, Yemonja is an òrìsà that supplicants do not put offerings or blood on. When making ebo to her, a stone from her icon is removed and that stone is given blood. Usually, the items that she prefers inside her icon are omi (water) and oti (gin). If one is to present flowers to Yemonja Awoyo Doyin (another òrìkì of Yemonja) never give her elebue, which are purple flowers, as they are taboo to her (Freeman, 2019).

While Yemonja is the mother of many òrìsà, she is closely associated with Sàngö as his adopted mother. Many Odu Ifá discuss the relationship that these two powerful òrìsà share. Their bond is almost inseparable as that of any mother and son. It is said that Yemonja is the only òrìsà who is powerful enough to carry the mighty òrìsà of thunder and lightning on her back. While Yorúbà culture is patriarchal, no man, regardless of how powerful they are, can "rule" without the consent of his mother or the elder mothers in many traditional African societies. In this instance, there is gender balance and respect among the sexes. No man can be more than his mother. It is mother who gives birth to man, nurtures him, and shows him the mysteries of cultural, political, economic, and spiritual power.

While not exhaustive this has been a brief introduction of Yemonja worship in Yorùbàland. Yemonja's importance to Yorùbá civilization as one of the ever-present mothers who literally births civilization by giving life to humans, animals, plants, and òrìsà. Most cities in the world are founded on major rivers, which are her dominion. Many of her followers were captured and enslaved in the Americas. While they were in the hellish conditions aboard those ships, the top layer of the Atlantic Ocean, owned by Olokun became a sort of world river. The rocking of the boats, to the Yorùbà on those vessels, was like that of a mother rocking her children, ever protecting them even as they experienced the horrors of the Maafa. Even now, for Yemonja worshippers especially in the Americas, we may pay homage to her at the ocean. For while she is Arugbo Odo, the most senior river òrìsà, she is also Okere Okun, the one who pays homage to the ocean. For this, we hail our great mother, Omi oooo.

REFERENCES

Freeman, Naja. 2019. Unpublished Personal Interview by Eric M. Bridges. Atlanta, GA. July 15, 2019.

Lugo, Nathan. 2019. Panel Discussion on Orisa Worship. Atlanta, GA. October 5, 2019.

Olayiwola, Ifakayode Faniyi. 2019. Unpublished Personal Interview by Eric M. Bridges. Atlanta, GA. October 30, 2019.

Chapter 2

Yemonja and the Dark Waters of the Unconscious

Reflections on an Africana Archetype

Tarrell Kyles

I have always had a great fear and respect for water, particularly large bodies of water. I can remember having recurring dreams of being washed away by enormous waves or being pursued by various underwater denizens as I sank into the depths. It was only in my late twenties, with the aid of African-centered spiritual study and practice, that I began to even remotely comprehend my internal-external (consistent with my study and training in indigenous psychologies, I conceptualize internal-external as a matter of simultaneous and shifting perspectives rather than separate phenomena) relationship with water, its imminence and vastness, its strength, its softness, and its demands of vulnerability. I came to understand its relationship to the moon, to fertility, and most importantly here, to the feminine. As I began to study and train in psychology, I came to understand these associations as archetypal.

The concept of the archetype is well known, both in psychological circles and within the mainstream of social consciousness. Though the concept is generally attributed to Carl Jung and located within his theoretical framework for analytical or depth psychology, noted scholars such as Dr. Edward Bynum (Bynum 2012) and Jungian analyst Dr. Fanny Brewster (Brewster 2017) have illuminated the ways in which Jung, and indeed psychology as a discipline, has drawn from the cultural consciousness of Africana peoples. Jung suggested that archetypes were the primordial, structural elements of the human psyche, complex symbols, which, taken together, constitute patterns and generative aspects of human thought and behavior. Despite Jung's insistence on the acultural nature of archetypes, contemporary scholarship has begun to examine the cultural implications of these concepts. This reflection contributes to the discourse by focusing on the Africana archetype of Yemonja. It begins with an introduction to Yemonja as the archetypal mother and divine feminine. Subsequently, it examines Yemonja's correlations with and relationship to the psyche and cultural consciousness of Africana peoples, and concludes with some insights into what these correlations and relationships could mean regarding the mental health and well-being of Africana peoples. This essay is in no way intended to reduce the Orisha to Western psychology's conceptualization of archetypes. Rather, it is a reflection upon the archetypal dimensions of Yemonja.

Yemonja, sometimes alternatively spelled Yemoja, is a feminine deity who emerges within the collective cultural consciousness of the Yoruba people. The Yoruba, who are mainly concentrated in Nigeria, but can also be found in areas of Benin and northern Togo, conceptualize Yemonja as Yeye (mother), omo (child/children), eja (fish), or the "mother whose children are the fish" (Canson 2014). It is Yemonja whose characteristically long breasts have not only nursed and nurtured many of the other Orisa (deities) but provided and continue to provide the primordial and generative aspects of humanity and human consciousness. In this aspect, the concept of fertility is emblematic of Yemonja.

Yemonja is a mother goddess. She is the great mother of all waters and thus the mother of terrestrial life, the fish, the "big mama" of the Orisha. These deities not only are aspects of the metaphysical, epistemological, and cosmological realities of Africana peoples but also serve a psychological function as archetypes, which emerge from the collective cultural consciousness of Africana peoples.

When we speak of the unconscious, we place ourselves within the framework of psychoanalysis as interpreted in the West, principally via the formulations of Sigmund Freud, Carl Jung, and others. Whereas the oldest orthodox Freudian conceptualization of the unconscious refers to the core of the mind functioning, in an explanatory sense, as the nucleus of individual thought, and shaped by social and cultural forces, Jung conceptualized the unconscious as being comprised of both a personal and a collective dimension (Day and Lau 2010, 101–119). Within Jung's formulation of the psyche we also find the concept of the archetypes, the Greek arche-tipos, or origin of patterns which theoretically comprise the embryonic template for human thought and behavior. Comparatively, African and other indigenous systems of thought and behavior have conceived of these archetypes as self-evident gods and goddesses, their functions and patterns expressed in terms of stories (both oral and written), as well as vivifying rituals, living cosmologies, and vast mythologies.

In mythologies throughout history and within various human cultures and civilizations we find evidence linking the concept of the unconscious with the archetypal element of water. The psyche and cultural consciousness of Africana peoples paradoxically yet simultaneously sustains Yemonja and is sustained by her, in intimate relationship, reflective of the mother-child dialectic. Within the African depths of the human psyche we find elucidations of water as generative, life giving, life sustaining, and in its absence and excess sometimes destructive, but ultimately life altering. Much like the unconscious mind, with her shifting tides, alternating between moments of deep rest and reflection, and spontaneous eruptions of creativity and psychic activity when she washes up on the shores of the conscious mind in the form of dreams, and slips of the tongue; the tides of large bodies of earthen water wax and wane with the lunar cycles, washing life and its remnants ashore, and away again into her depths.

Within her work, "Stepping into Forest: Incorporating the Lost Girl Back into Self" (Johnson 2017, 85), doctoral candidate, Alisa Orduña directs our attention to the ancient connection between the unconscious and the sea as she courageously embarks on her journey into more intimate interrelationship with psyche and realizes, "I was facing the West—the land of the unconscious, and the holder of my truth." Within Hermetic-Alchemical, Western Esoteric, and many indigenous traditions, the West has been commonly associated with the element of water, of the realm of emotions, and the providence of the Divine Feminine.

The African worldview, like many indigenous worldviews, not only foregrounds the primacy of spirit but also accepts the multidimensional nature of reality, not as an abstraction but as lived and experiential. In this worldview, the spiritual and the material are not separate, but are rather, interrelated aspects of divinity. Relatedly, the archetype of the Divine Feminine can in this way be approached as being as vast and complex as the earthly oceans we find on the material plane of existence. While she holds space for the life-giving processes and sustenance often associated with mothering, she also encompasses shadow, lunar associations and cyclical patterns, emotions (ranging from the most filtered to the rawest and perhaps most powerful), and sexuality. The archetype of the Divine Feminine also draws various associations, both ancient and contemporary, with many aspects of earthly material womanhood, ranging from rites of passage concerning the flow of time and development from female childhood, on into middle and older age, as well as ovulation, and menstruation.

"Yemaya is the calm blue waters of the South Pacific and the raging tidal wave" (Omilade 2003, 30–31). Like all of the Orisha, the Africana archetypes, Yemonja's manifestations are myriad and dynamic. In the *Handbook of Yoruba Religious Concepts*, Baba Ifa Karade venerates Yemaya as,

> the divinity of all oceans. She is said to be the mother of all orisha and expresses her mothering throughout the earthly and heavenly realms. Yemoja is the

matriarchal head of the cosmic universe. She is the amniotic fluid in the womb of the pregnant woman, as well as, the breasts which nurture. She is known to be very stern and temperamental and expresses the protective energies of the feminine force. (Karade 1994, 26–27)

Globally, practitioners and students of Africana healing systems from Vodun, and Ifa, to Lukumi and even African American Hoodoo (root work and conjure) understand themselves and the communities they serve through the archetypal lens of forces like Yemonja.

In all of its psychocultural varieties, both ancient and contemporary, human imagination has and continues to regard fluidity, formlessness, darkness, emotions, and the feminine as mysterious. Both biologically and mythologically, from the bodily womb to the earthly tomb, the Divine Feminine represents the gateway between the realm of the living and the visible, and the realm of the underworld and the invisible. When passing from being in utero to terrestrial life, what may we be forgetting in terms of consciousness? With the exception of some schools of thought like depth psychology, which posit theories of the unconscious as the psychological repository for that which is in some sense forgotten, the Western view may look to tie this provocation into a neatly bound empirical knot. However, the African worldview, with spirit as its generative principle, might instead propose that, that which the West conceives of as unconscious, is in fact, ancestral, and accessible via indigenous methodologies, provided that we allow ourselves to be in living relationship with what the contemporary world may regard as both invisible and mysterious.

It is important to note some of the nuances of African thought regarding Yemonja, primordial waters, and mystery. Dr. Fanny Brewster, in her recounting of an analysand's dream as interpreted by a Yoruban Babalawo, provokes and complicates Western understandings of the psyche and gender. Dr. Brewster explains that her analysand, Rae, dreamt of an 8- to 10-year-old boy who was pulling and picking away at a sponge that was growing from his right upper chest. The sponge, described by Rae as being blue and rectangular with a black backing, kept growing back no matter how many times it was removed. Within the dream, Rae suggested to a woman, possibly the boy's mother, that they should try a homeopathic method in order to treat it from the inside and keep it from growing back. Rae was especially unsettled by the mysterious and resistant nature of the sponge. The Babalawo, Baba Adetunde attributed the dream to Yemonja in an especially nuanced manner. "Baba Adetunde, in looking at the above dream by Rae, saw the image of Olukun, orisa of the ocean. He said that it was a 'beautiful' dream. In The Way of the Orisha, Neimark described Olukun: In Africa, Yemonja is represented by the Ogun River rather than by the top layer of the ocean as she is in the New

World. Olukun has come to reflect the bottom or mysterious part of the ocean . . . It is here that secrets are preserved and kept, that the unknown is knowable, and that riches and treasures of the world abound" (Neimark 1993, 118). "According to Baba Adetunde, the dream holds all the energy of the ocean goddess Yemonja or Olukun. The boy is actually one of her children from the sea. The fact that they both appear in Rae's dream highlights her favored status with this goddess. The blue of the sponge is natural to the blue of the ocean. Sponges grow in the ocean. All the dream elements indicated to Baba Adetunde the presence of Olukun and Rae's favored status with this goddess because she is being employed in her service" (Brewster 2017, 42).

Baba Adetunde's interpretation of the dream raises the interesting paradox of the masculine within the feminine, as in some interpretations, Olukun is a masculine deity or archetype, manifesting as the depths to Yemonja's oscillating waves. The realization of Yemonja and Olukun as perhaps not only one, but as goddess, or feminine divinity calls our attention to the spiritual and psychological limitations of the Western concept of gender as it is applied or perhaps misapplied to Africana peoples. Perhaps the relational dynamics of Yemonja and Olukun are themselves, emblematic of the mystery inherent within the Dark Waters of the Africana cultural consciousness in general and its unconscious realms in particular. There is an ever-present opportunity for the mystery to extend and amplify itself when it can be engaged within its own cultural context, as opposed to being imported into Western contexts and dissected for empirical (perhaps imperial) digestion. Despite Western patriarchal thought's preoccupation with penetration, with "demystifying," and penetrating the mysteries (penetrating the Divine Feminine?), and going "where no man has gone before," Yemonja's watery depths, much like the unconscious mind, embody a kind of impenetrability, recalling the wide spread indigenous belief that spirit(s) can pass through solid matter, but not through water. Yemonja remains eternal, sustaining and altering psychic and material life, waxing and waning with the lunar and feminine cycles of life, attending those who engage her on her terms, to their own strength, vulnerability, creativity, and adaptability. It is to this notion of adaptability that we turn lastly as we reflect upon how Yemonja may become part of how we might better understand ourselves, our environment and each other as we entrust ourselves to the living work of healing all three.

Though I am a student and scholar of indigenous Africana psychologies, I am not a formally initiated Babalawo (traditional priest in the Yoruba Ifa system), so, as part of my process for constructing this piece I began to ponder, heart first, the ways in which I could communicate how the Divine Feminine as Yemonja could aid in our healing and liberation. What emerged for me was the notion that we might begin by first recognizing, reembracing, and reintegrating the feminine within ourselves regardless of our sex and sexuality. We might also begin our work by appreciating women, mystery, and femininity broadly in all of their manifestations. This also entails reengagements with that which is ancient, spiritual and sacred. The destruction of indigenous peoples and cultures globally, as a consequence of European expansion in the form of genocide, enslavement, and colonialism, has, along with its material harms, been heavily focused upon, what Africana psychiatrist, philosopher, and decolonial theorist Frantz Fanon referred to as, "violence beyond violence" (Nobles 2015, 42). In keeping with the Africana cultural consciousness, Fanon conceived of "violence beyond violence" as an *invisible* destructive force which among other things, asserts and maintains that the European is the universal standard for human thought and behavior. Africana psychologist Wade Nobles cautions that "when African people accept a system of values and norms as universal which removes the African from the stage of human history, this results in a distortion of the African psyche that is devastating" (Nobles 2015, 43). In large part, the devastation results in a kind of shattering or fragmenting of the Africana psyche, forcing Africana peoples to lead lives divorced from the deepest aspects of ourselves, as well as our families and communities, divorcing us from any meaningful relationships with the land, as well as our own deepest wounds and desires. Welcoming the sacred, the spiritual, and the mysteries of the Divine Feminine back into our lives may be one of the most essential tasks put before Africana peoples in terms of our healing and inevitable liberation. In keeping with this line of thought, attuning to femininity and seeking to be in relationship and work with Yemonja presents possibilities for healing outside of the dominant Western paradigm. Yemonja in her role as the Divine Feminine can help guide us, individually and collectively, through the depths of our more hidden psychological and spiritual challenges, toward safer waters, helping us to make the unconscious, conscious, so that we might live fuller, more aware, more sustainable, and most importantly, whole (no longer fragmented) lives.

Additionally, reentering into active relationship with Yemonja as the Divine Feminine may aid Africana peoples in becoming aware of and attending to our own individual and collective grief. After all, would it not be wise to begin addressing the immeasurable grief of being stripped of one's mother tongue, mother cultures, and motherland by reconstructing one's relationship with the archetypal divine mother? In this regard, Fanny Brewster reminds us that

> There has been a historical deprecation of African countries as well as the enslaved Africanist birth mothers who were separated from their children. The importance of remembering an imaginal African psyche in all its beauty and with all of its potentiality is necessary. It is important to remember that

African Americans had and can claim that place of the African motherland—as a location in the Africanist psyche as seen by Africanist cultural consciousness. (Brewster 2017, 64)

In her more recent work, *Archetypal Grief: Slavery's Legacy of Intergenerational Child Loss*, Brewster examines the "conscious and unconscious grief and sorrow" of Africana women due to the inhumane world created by the use of genocide, enslavement, and colonialism by Europeans. In light of new research emerging within neuroscience and neuropsychology, we are able to deepen the ways in which we understand archetypes and the unconscious, these ways lend a kind of Western credence to what indigenous psychologies have long known about ancestral memory, the emotional body, and other aspects of human consciousness related to elements of the Divine Feminine. Brewster suggests that we very seriously consider "the influence of archetypal mother-goddess energy," and look toward Yemonja in particular, as she is not only "the goddess who protects mothers and watches over children" (Brewster 2017, 11) but she is the archetypal energy of the Divine Feminine within many African-centered spiritual systems throughout the diaspora. As we currently and collectively inhabit a time-space in which women in general and Africana women in particular, are reawakening to the power of the Divine Feminine within them, it seems providential that as Africana peoples we would join together in the spirit of the times and embrace Yemonja.

In *The Unknown She: Eight Faces of an Emerging Consciousness* Hilary Hart dialogues with author, healer, and keeper of her peoples' sacred ways Sobonfu Somé. Somé explains to Hart that her purpose is to confront the destruction of indigenous peoples and their worlds, to keep the rituals of her peoples alive, and to do so in a woman's way. Somé reminds us to embody Yemonja's adaptability like the women of her village toward shapeshifting or being able to "use energy in many different ways" (Hart 2003). Much of Somé's work revolves around guiding both men and women in developing their feminine qualities toward self-transformation as well as aiding the Divine Feminine to heal and grow in our contemporary time-space. Finally, regarding the Divine Feminine, Somé offers that, "Feminine spirit works in different ways. Its foundation is that it sustains everything, it weaves things together, it maintains harmony, it comes with intuition. It affirms life, recognizes and sees value in individuals. It can be a strong barrier to negative influences, especially in a community." She continues, invoking our earlier reflections upon the invisible and the mysterious "Feminine power is different from masculine power because you cannot see it so clearly" (Hart 2003, 236). "The one that is *hidden* [emphasis mine] can achieve a lot more than the one that is out there." Somé reminds us that "Unconsciously we know we have feminine spirit; it lives inside us, and it is important to consciously honor and appreciate it" (Hart 2003, 237).

Perhaps, if within U.S.-born Africana communities and throughout the diaspora we can enliven and reintegrate the deep and archetypal dimensions of ourselves (our African selves as inseparable from an African cultural consciousness which encompasses and extends outward as family, community, world, and cosmos) we may experience a transformation of psyche which could bring us into more intimate harmony and relationship with our inner depths, each other, and our external environments.

REFERENCES

Brewster, F. 2017. *African Americans and Jungian Psychology: Leaving the Shadows*. London: Routledge.

———. 2018. *Archetypal Grief: Slavery's Legacy of Intergenerational Child Loss*. London: Routledge.

Bynum, E. B. 2012. *The African Unconscious*. New York: Cosimo, Inc.

Canson, Patricia E. 2014. "Yemonja." In *Encylopedia Britannica*, Accessed October 6, 2018. https://www.britannica.com/topic/Yemonja.

Day, R. E., and Lau, A. J. 2010. "Psychoanalysis as Critique in the Works of Freud, Lacan, and Deleuze and Guattari." In *Critical Theory for Library and Information Science: Exploring the Social from Across the Discipline*, edited by Leckie et al. Santa Barbara: Libraries Unlimited, 101–119.

Karade, B. I. 1994. *The Handbook of Yoruba Religious Concepts*. Newburyport: Weiser Books.

Nobles, W. W. 2015. *The Island of Memes: Haiti's Unfinished Revolution*. Baltimore, MD: Black Classic Press.

Omilade Iyalorisha Correal, T. M. 2003. *Finding Soul on the Path of Orișa: A West African Spiritual Tradition*. New York: Crossing Press.

Orduña, Alisa. 2017. "Stepping into Forest: Incorporating the Lost Girl Back into Self." In *Seeing in the Dark: Wisdom Works by Black Women in Depth Psychology*, edited by Sharon D. Johnson. New York: Malibu Press, 80–85.

Chapter 3

Iyemonja, Omi Jori

Our Mother, Leader of the Waters

Iya Osundamisi Fafunke

I don't intend to sound as though I am xeroxing the mood of the late Virginia Woolf in her acclaimed narrative *A Room of One's Own*, yet I can't resist mentioning the unforeseeable drawbacks I envisioned when asked to write a chapter in a publication about a female deity. In a land where the powers that be most often express the idea that spiritual hierarchy equates to maleness, I courageously accepted the challenge. The concept of religion itself leaves the reader with perplexing wonder about unresolved mysteries surrounding the absolute gender of GOD. The need to come to any agreement around the subject can present resistance toward the tolerance of feminine power and potentiality among female spirits.

In this chapter, I am discussing the West African deity, Iyemonja or most often referred to as Yemoja. Iyemonja is understood to translate as mother of mermaids/fish, hence she is often depicted as half human and half fish in various West African art forms. In West African Yoruba traditional religion, she is worshipped among several water deities. It is normal for such deities to be directly associated with one or more elements of nature. Yemoja is considered the principle water deity or elder of the rivers which is why she is called omo jori-leader of the waters. She holds the highest rank in terms of her age among other river deities. The reason why these spirits are spoken about as if they share human characteristics is because they do. According to the late Ayo Salami, primordial deities came to earth and lived according to the functions which the highest power sent them to perform. (We will discuss this highest power later.) This included forming human life, harvesting crops, and solving problems among the other deities. Salami's research reveals that all of the deities had been living on Earth among humans at some point. It is understood that the deities only separated themselves into the heavenly realm when it was shown that humans refused to give proper recognition to the deities for their good deeds (Salami 2008).

I had an opportunity to interview an Orisa priest and high chief known as Chief Aikula Oluwin-Oosa or Nathan Lugo of Miami, Florida. He suggested that we call Yemonja, the deity/goddess okere okun because she can go straight to ocean or sea without paying homage to other river deities along the path. The other river deities in fact must pay her homage (Lugo 2018). Her river is called the Ogun river and is the most ancient of all rivers. It is the longest river in Yoruba land. In terms of the functions she was assigned to perform, she is highly associated with child bearing—the process of giving birth to children, while Osun (another water deity) is the fertility deity for ensuring barren mothers are able to conceive and become pregnant with child. She is also known for her assistance in the areas of wealth, abundancy, victory over enemies, arts and crafts, pottery making, healing of the sick and wounded, and much more. Yemoja is prominent and respected. She is the one who brings all the water deities and rivers together. An interview with a high chief in Osogbo, Osun State, Nigeria, known as Baba Agbongbon Kayode Olayiwola Faniyi revealed that is why we greet her as omi ooo. To help me understand some of the nature of Yemoja, he taught me one poem that the Yoruba call oriki. Oriki is a collection of praises given to a particular deity based on his or her likes, dislikes, attributes and more. The oriki goes as follows:

Yemoja Ti mese lodo Yemonja
O je eye etu
O je pepeye
the one who lives inside the river
the one who loves to eat guinea fowl
the one who loves to eat duck
ki o gba Alubosa ki o fi ro efo
Yemoja Yee
Come and receive these onions from me in order to prepare your green vegetables
Praises to Yemoja

(Ifaniyi 2017)

There are many images of Yemoja floating around as a nursing mother with long breasts. Most internet sources or wood carvings will include this particular artistry. The reason for this is that she is seen as being the source of life. The birth of children is a joyful occasion for Yoruba people. All of the nourishment needed in order for a child to survive inside and outside of the womb is said to be provided by Yemoja.

It would be advantageous to shine more light on the West African Orisa tradition as it pertains to the acknowledgement and worship of the deities.

Often, onlookers have deemed the religion of the Yoruba as polytheistic because they worship various deities called Orisa. However, the Yoruba do not view their spiritual practices as polytheistic at all. In Kobi Kambon's *African/Black Psychology in the American Context*, he shares Cheikh Diop's earlier expression that the African or Southern Cradle of the world believes in one universal God. He further describes manifestations of African religious expression and practices as recognition/acknowledgement to God as the supreme being; the Creator's presence and the ancestors' spiritual presence as a regular part of life activities (Kambon 1998). I agree with Diop that the Yoruba religion is monotheistic. It is the manner of worshipping God that determines whether or not a religion is monotheistic (worshipping one god) or polytheistic (worshipping of multiple gods). Through the years that I have studied and taught about religious structures, I am convinced that the existence of deities other than God as in the West African Yoruba religion does not make it polytheistic. According to some, there are one thousand four hundred Yoruba deities called Orisa. Orisa are sources that are summoned when one does not have what is required for them to live a full life (money, children, spouse, good health, etc.).

In Olodumare, God in Yoruba belief, Idowu said that the Yorubas' attitude or concept of God referred to as Olodumare is that they owe their entire existence to God and that God portioned out the theocratic administration of the world among the many primordial Yoruba divinities/deities (Idowu 1994). Olodumare can be translated to mean the owner of the heavens among Yoruba-speaking people. The Orisa, held a subordinate position to God in the spiritual realm. All necessary tasks required to establish earth and its inhabitants were carried out by the Orisa at the direction of God. In accordance with Yemonja's extraordinary ability to solve earth's and humans' day-to-day problems, she is among the notable deities in the Yoruba pantheon.

It is believed that the divinities have special powers attributed to each of them. Later, I will attempt to show a comparison of what West African traditional worshippers believe about Yemonja's contributions to human life to what followers in the diaspora believe to be her powers and attributes. Furthermore, the Yoruba people seem to believe that all dealings in heaven and on earth are controlled by the deities. Therefore, it appears that there is no separation between the humans and the deities—meaning that they are completely devoted to them. This is seen in their daily worship of the deities through what is called ose days. Each deity has its own identified ose day. On these days, depending on the deities assigned to the day, prayers and offerings are offered accordingly. The Yoruba calendar is based on a four-day rotation. Every four days, specific deities/orisa are highlighted by Yoruba religion practitioners all around the world. While some of the rituals and protocols involved in specific worship may differ, they all share common practices as

it relates to the process of communication and making offerings to the deities. Yemoja, in particular, will receive an overwhelming energetic transfer
through offerings of gin, green vegetables, onions, pounded yam, and corn
pudding.

After collecting accounts from various subjects pertaining to their understanding of the nature of Yemoja, their responses were not shocking at all. I
will make a fair and unprejudiced attempt to demonstrate that these perceptions diminish the influence of the feminine divine on spiritual hierarchy
and limits the robustness of individuals and groups' spiritual development
and deliberation. A series of questionnaires given to both ordained and non-
ordained Yoruba Orisa priests from various backgrounds revealed some
interesting perspectives on the purpose or function of Yemoja in the lives
of followers. Responses were coded based on the nature of the function or
identified attributes of Yemoja. Most were characterized by stereotypes commonly associated with women in roles which are deemed sexist or gender-
biased. One recurring theme was descriptions of her in the most docile and
passive women's roles. I refer to this as "putting Yemoja in her place";
included in submitted descriptions were:

• Nurturing
• Motherly
• Elderly woman
• Protector of women and children

Another strong indicator of "putting Yemoja in her place" throughout
diasporic practices involves the food items offered to her during worship and
appeasement. For example, many Western recipes for Yemoja food include
molasses syrup. Molasses is a very rich and sweet substance often poured in
the river or on her shrine icons in certain diasporic traditions. However, in
Yoruba land, molasses is not among the offerings for Yemoja. In fact, green
vegetables and onions are the staple food items offered to her in exchange for
spiritual favor from her. The sweetness of molasses further places restrictions
on her existence because it implies that Yemoja is agreeable or saccharine. I
am not refuting her sentimental and delightful nature. I am simply stating that
she cannot only be reduced to that. For example, the bitterness of the onion
that we offer her is indicative of one's offenses toward her or her followers
are resentful in nature and can result in personal disturbance.

The manifestation of gender norms and roles in society is an age-old
dilemma that spills over into the realm of the feminine divine-the female spir-
its/deities. The result is a collective of stereotypical and obscured understandings of the presence and purpose of feminine deities such as Yemoja. It is
necessary to discuss briefly the sexual politics related to constructing gender

norms in society. It is clear that gender discrimination and bias is the new racism because it upholds inequality among women in society. Potentially, the African woman's agency is compromised due to her nature being depicted as overly sexual, extremely docile, weak, and helpless among others. "Her treatment helped create modern black sexual stereotypes of the jezebel, the mammy, and the welfare queen, that in the United States help uphold slavery, Jim Crow segregation, and racial ghettoization" (Collins 2005). Therefore, it's not at all surprising that female deities, particularly Yemoja, have been plagued with similar labels—especially the mammy portrayal. When participants of the questionnaires were asked to elaborate on the description of her as the elderly woman few hesitated to explain that she was like the grandmother of the other Orisa, or that she was like their grandmother. With limited understanding of what that meant, I took it further by searching for images of her in the media. In comparison to other female deities, Yemoja was often portrayed as older with less appealing physical traits. As opposed to one of her junior deities, Osun, Yemonja's skin was darker and was usually dressed in colonial style, floor length dresses. On the contrary, other female deities were painted in revealing clothing, long natural hair and more Eurocentric features. Furthermore, a narrow observation of Western pictorial expressions available revealed that Yemoja among other female deities are associated deeply with female body parts such as enlarged, voluptuous breasts which are in direct contrast of African art that show Yemonja as a figure with saggy breast, a natural occurrence for nursing mothers.

Overall, the fleshy images created and consumed by Westerners often accentuate the buttocks, hips, and thighs—seemingly piquing the interest in African women's sexuality rather than her spirituality. Unfortunately, the redundant sexual renditions of the African women create a permanence of gender racism that has the potential to influence future generations. These gender constructs in society highlight what bell hooks refers to as psychological patriarchy. She explains that psychological patriarchy creates a misperception that men are the enemy—especially to feminists, but but also to themselves. She states that to end male pain or male crises we have to work to end patriarchy (hooks 2004). This is relevant because when it comes down to male pain and suffering, men should not feel threatened and be open to tapping into divine feminine energy for healing. In other words, it would be advantageous to understand that Orisa Yemoja is more than a spirit associated with child-bearing among other gender-biased roles.

Her contribution to restoring the lives of her devotees are timeless and eloquent. If practitioners are not encouraged to teach more balanced information about Yemoja, we risk the lack of inspiration for more men to come forward and worship her or become initiated as Yemoja priests. I have experienced novice devotees questioning, on being told they should worship Yemoja, if it is a "woman thing." Specifically, they would ask, "Can men be initiated to Yemoja since she is a female deity?" I have also witnessed men who are initiated to feminine deities display feminine gestures (seductive swerving of the hips) when worshipping, singing, and dancing to certain songs containing female deities' liturgy. Some may even clothe themselves in women's clothes, skirts, etc., when attending worship ceremonies. It is quite perplexing that men see representing and worshipping feminine deities through the lens of psychological patriarchy, and that they must hide any behavior normally related to maleness. It is my belief that what I am describing is a conflict between what it means to be feminine and masculine and how it determines the way certain deities are worshiped.

There could be a fine line drawn between spirituality and sexism. In order to evolve spiritually, we must draw the line and break the social taboos that separate us from reaching our higher selves. The priesthood of any Orisa comes about because the human's natural instinct is to be in tune with the supernatural world.

Male or female, woman or man, the role of the priest is to be the mediator between spirits and humans. Such mediation must be characterized with the willingness to dismantle Western beliefs about gender. Male priests of Yemoja must accept the role as warrior as eloquently as they accept the role of child bearer and vice versa. According to Oyewunmi, "Gender was not an organizing principle in Yoruba society prior to colonization by the West. She further indicated that the primary principle of social organizations was seniority, defined by relative age" (Oyewumni 1997). This is highly critical as it luminates Yemoja's position as the elder and leader among all other water deities. Whenever we chant "Omi O" we are acknowledging her premise in regards to seniority.

The trouble with Western thought on gender is that it often places one (men) higher on the hierarchy over the other (women). Yoruba thought does not prescribe to this ideology which often leads to male privilege. Oyewunmi states that the Yoruba terms "Obinrin" and "Okunrin" are often mistranslated to mean female/woman and male/man in English. She indicated that the common suffix *rin* suggests a common humanity (Oyewumni 1997). This lessens the subordination and powerlessness among the spectrum of women or feminine beings. The terms only refer to the physicality of the beings rather than their hierarchy in Yoruba society. This is due to the need to make distinctions for the sake of intercourse and procreation. Outside of that, the binary explanation of either does not give us differential descriptions of powers or functionality beyond that. There is an urgent need for an overwhelming overhaul on our way of thinking about female deities. The whole point here is that gender constructs and the understanding of gender identity do not act alone within cultural paradigms. These categories are embedded in how we envision our worship of specific Yoruba deities. Unfortunately, the mislabeling of gender identities among Yoruba deities causes a significant decrease in benefits for the practitioners.

We must step away from this gender identification of Orisa and accept that Orisa have their own unbiased identities. Orisa identity is simply the attributes, likes, dislikes, and functions highly associated with a particular deity. With the Yoruba pantheon and with the correct knowledge of Orisa identity, everyone can secure longevity, health and wellness, children, wealth, victory over calamities, etc. Furthermore, the functional premise of which Yemoja exist can no longer be misconstrued. An overwhelming 76 percent of respondents indicated that their perception of Yemoja was that of a motherly and nurturing figure. Indeed, Yemoja is celebrated among the Yoruba and its descendants as the mother of many sorts. Like one of her popular counterparts, Orisa Osun, Yemoja is also considered by her followers as the giver of children to barren women. I thought it would be very important to make some distinctions here so that both deities are given their own individual identities as it pertains to their prescribed duties among the Yoruba pantheon. According to Baba Fakayode Faniyi and Nathan Lugo, she is precisely sought after and venerated when a mother is attempting to conceive.

She can also be seen as a mother in a different aspect. Ye Mo N Eja, the *mother* of fish speaks to her role as a provider of abundant wealth. The worshipper of Yemoja will never lack and will always have an abundance of resources, according to sources. This can be easily noticed by the string of cowries included in her shrine icon. Cowry shells, are known to be one of the earlier forms of currency in the ancient world. It is said that there is no water source be it river, lake, stream or ocean that does not contain an abundance of fish. Even as many are removed from the water source through any unimaginable incident, many are reformed or replenished. That is the nature of Yemoja, the mother of fish.

There were only few respondents who indicated that they sought Yemoja for wealth and prosperity. Given the breakdown and meaning of her name, it was shocking that only 1 percent viewed her a provider of wealth and abundancy. One of the least responses regarding Yemoja's purpose in the lives of practitioners and devotees was her very few respondents viewed Yemonja's role as a warrior or protector. Jagun ti awon odo (warrior of the river) is included in the many praise names recited in her honor. The fact of the matter is that Yemoja's military style capabilities sets her apart from other female deities. The goddess is adequately equipped to engage war against the enemies of her followers. This can be determined by the tools included in her icons of worship. Included among these articles are various shaped cutlasses. Historically, cutlasses were used on land, yet they were common naval weapons for soldiers of the waters. I argue that it is not a coincidence that the tools exist in her vessel. Yemoja is characterized with the nature of defending her devotees in acts of war or spiritual warfare if necessary. It is also to be noted here that cutlasses were also used on land in ancient times in order to assist farmers with cultivating crops. Although I have not learned of any association between Yemoja and farming, it may be inferred that her role in providing abundancy and resources for her worshippers can be related to the cutlasses included in her shrine icons.

I wanted to explore Yemonja's role in the realm of witchcraft or sorcery. It is interesting that less than 1 percent of the questionnaire participants responded that their understanding of Yemoja was associated with what we may call wizardry. Yet those of us who know, understand that Yemoja is in fact the one that kills one's enemy and manifests the curse in order to do so. She inherits the skill of wizardry. Many have attempted to associate her with the Yoruba group we call the Iyami, or spiritual mothers of the deep darkness. These entities are considered very powerful and most humans fear their presence in both the physical and supernatural world. The Iyami are consulted mainly for offenses against women. They are known to have the power to render destruction and demise to any suspecting offender of women's well-being, peace, and inclination to prosper. Iyami, known to wander at night in order to pluck the organs inside out of unsuspecting victims, enforce a horrifying submission to their rule. Some have stated that Yemoja is the leader of the Iyami sorority. Other female deities have also been named to hold the same position. To align Yemoja with the Iyami can be damaging in a sense that it can potentially deter reverence to her circle of worship. However, it should not induce such a negative impact on believers. Still I was taught an interesting fact about Yemoja's affiliation with malevolent spirits such as Iyami. According to Nathan Lugo, Yemoja is closely associated with wizardry which is why we call her Jogun Oso—the one who inherits curse or wizardry (Lugo 2018). When Ye Ye (a Yoruba term of endearment referring to one's mother) becomes angered, those in her path shall feel a mighty wrath. Don't take her gentility for weakness.

The chief priest also explained that she has the ability to be present at any place-river, ocean etc., which speaks to her majestic abilities. She can flow or go straight to the sea without paying homage to any other of the many water deities who refer to her leadership among other water deities. Of importance is how we satisfy the spiritual essence of Yemoja. Part of her list of items when offering gifts is the guinea fowl, we call etu in Yoruba land. I found it intriguing that the only sure method of distinguishing the sex of the guinea fowl is by the noise it makes, unlike most chickens, the guinea fowl cannot be sexed at hatch. There is no physical marking to tell the female from the male. This bird, with its West African origins and mysterious nature, was most helpful in forming an impression of Yemoja minus the gender constructs and reinforces Oyewunmi's assertions about gender mentioned earlier in this chapter.

There is a direct correlation between the limited knowledge of her energy and the limited access or purpose of her worship. Narrow perceptions of Yemoja and other feminine deities shape worshippers' expectations of their own spiritual fulfillment. Individuals and groups hope to gain existence, merit, purpose, resources and meaning of life by worshipping spirits. Her importance must not be diminished by stereotypes as they only restrict her spiritual essence and divinity. The deities' identity can only be traced to her attributes and aid to human life. It is what she represents spiritually, and not her appearance or social constructs that inform her relevance in our lives. What I certainly attempt to do here is to challenge the existing conditions on how we understand and approach Orisa Yemoja. Any type of misinformation related to Yemoja or any African deities leads to the alienation of the African spirit and results in the uncertainty of how Orisa function in our lives.

As I have indicated, most of the responses I received encased Yemoja's spiritual role as passive, docile, and even as an old maid; while respondents answered with their best intentions, it is important that they begin to see the many facets of Yemonja. She has a strong feminine existence. We call her "oteetee areyin pan Sango," the big strong woman who can carry Sango on her back. Sango is the Yoruba deity we have come to know as the powerful king. Imagine the scene of a dominant warrior man, large in stature. Imagine him as being wounded at war and having to be carried on the back of a woman. That is Yemoja—the one who is capable of this amazing feat. We have come to accept that Yemonja is the spiritual mother of Sango. That is why it is common to see Sango worshippers give offering to Yemonja when appeasing Sango.

Another noble mention regarding Yemoja is that she is closely associated with human creation. It is believed that she provided the water to wet the clay used for human formation in Yoruba origin stories. This speaks to her relationships with other orisa in the divine pantheon. Particularly here, I am referring to Obatala, the Orisa of the white cloth and the one that is understood to have formed and shaped human anatomy at the summon of Olodumare. She is also affiliated with Obatala because it has been mentioned before that use of the white cloth is predominate. So is the use of a whitened calabash to hold her spiritual icons. It shows that she nor any other deity stand alone in their contribution to human life and manifestations. So that we are clearer than the beads worn to represent the existence of Yemoja among the Yoruba, our mother is an extraordinary figure without limitations. The unassailable descriptions of her miraculous functions and leadership among other deities can move us all in the right direction for enjoying her prevalence throughout the universe. It is time to shift the narrative by offering truth. Rather than hiding in the shadow of distorted female goddess images, Yemoja has earned a place in the respectful and revered center of our existence.

REFERENCES

Collins, Patricia Hill. 2005. *Black Sexual Politics: African Americans, Gender, and the New Racism.* New York: Taylor and Francis Group.

Hooks, bell. 2004. *The Will to Change: Men, Masculinity, and Love.* New York: Atria Books.

Idowu, E. Bolaji. 1994. *Olodumare: God in Yoruba Belief.* New York: Wazobia.

Ifaniyi, Fakayode Olayiwola. 2017. Interviewed by Naja Freeman. *Chief,* June 25.

Kambon, Kobi. 1998. *African/Black Psychology in the American Context: An African Centered Approach.* Tallahassee: Nubian Nation.

Lugo, Nathan. 2018. Interview by Naja Freeman. *Chief,* December 2.

Oyewumni, Oyeronke. 1997. *The Invention of Women: Making an African Sense of Western Gender Discourses.* Minneapolis: University of Minnesota Press.

Salami, Ayo. 2008. *Yoruba Theology and Tradition: The Genealogy.* Lagos: NIDD Publishing Company Limited.

Chapter 4

Yemonja Braidings in Obeah Practices in the Anglophone Caribbean

Sandra Gonsalves-Domond

Throughout the slaveocracy traversing into post-colonialism, Obeah as a practice has been vilified through a racist and ethnocentric, Eurocentric lens. The plantocracy and colonial societies through their rapacious acts of barbarism, dispossessions, and nullification thoroughly propagandized and debased the African practice and practitioners as malevolent, violent, nefarious, and akin to demonic sorcery and witchcraft. These singular, colonial narratives propagated by powers of enforcement, permeated representations of Obeah as transgressive to the social order, threatening, and criminal to European imperialism in Anglophone islands such as Jamaica, Trinidad and Tobago, Barbados, and Antigua. Paradigm shifting with more Afro-diasporic prisms and reclaimed multicultural tools of analyses, Obeah has always had its rightful place in Indigenous African Religions and has been nurtured from its Yoruba roots and cosmology. As Jacob Olupona asserts in an interview recorded in the *Harvard Gazette*, these collective belief systems with their spiritual potency were plural, holistic, and threaded through the entire life spaces of their devotees—not separated out or compartmentalized in comparison to closed theological, codified systems like Christianity (Olupona 2015, 27). A central nub of the belief was the veneration of ancestors because they offered meaningful, progenitorial linkages to the living. Based on an oral tradition, Obeah was accommodating and inclusive of other ideas. Also, Obeah has taken its reverential place within the field of folklore studies as a tangible, evidentiary-based, authenticated history that Africanism survived in the region (Olupona 2015).

Moreover, Obeah has played an integral part in indigenous healing traditions and was weaponized as one tool in the military-resistance strategies toward the goals of liberation from hegemonic imperialism. With successes in the 1760 Tacky Slave Rebellion, 1823 Guinea Jack Boxing Day Conspiracy,

and famous Paul Bogle's 1865 Morant Bay rebellions in Jamaica, and cou-
pled with military victories of the Maroon heroine, Nanny, who mythically
rendered the bullets of the English ineffective with her rump, Obeah agitated
against, and politically challenged the social order in what Barima refers to
as "Jamaica's Black Resistance Hierarchy" (Barima 2016). He concludes
in *Cutting across Space and Time: Obeah's Service to Jamaica's Freedom
Struggle in Slavery and Emancipation* that colonial authorities were genu-
inely mortified by the powers of Obeah. "Its rituals, herbs, and other dimensions were effective tools for organizing, and *all* of Jamaica's major revolts
and revolutionary conspiracies occurred when *Obeah* was involved (Barima
2016, 15).

Given the verisimilitude and potency of these historical accounts, we must
surely revisit the heroine Nanny, also known as Grandy Nanny later on in
our discussion, as her acts elevated the revered spirit world of Yemonja as
the Feminine Divine circulating within the personage of this female Obeah-
woman. In this article, the healing Orisha Yemonja's beliefs are examined
within its proximity to Obeah practices in the Anglophone Caribbean,
demonstrating the nexus of Africanism and their continuity in the diaspora.
Secondly, this work will valorize qualitatively Black feminist epistemological knowledge constructions as the lens of analyses to consciously validate
this African goddess among the polytheistic belief systems from the African
continent. Eurocentric patriarchal beliefs are dismissive, irreverent, and mar-
ginalize the Female Divine. A third goal, is that, since there is a paucity of
research in the Feminine Divine, this is an attempt to springboard and revi-
talize erudite, scholarly interests in African-centered spiritual cosmology and
to make it more fecund, all pun intended, given that Yemonja is the goddess
of fertility.

It is acknowledged that there is a dearth of research that threads Yemonja
to Obeah in an isomorphically and historically chronological manner. This
attempt then, is to, examine elements of both traditions that are intersectional
from a twenty-first-century prism, and from what has either been supported
by oral traditions or codification, or both. In fact, the literature on Obeah has
witnessed scholarly growth over the past decades (Patton 2012; Fernández
and Paravisini-Gebert 2000; Payne-Jackson n.d.). Toxic masculinity strategies, yoked with virulent Eurocentric attempts at erasure of Afro-spiritual
practices, although sustained were unsuccessful, as Obeah practitioners
continued their healing traditions up to today in the Caribbean region and
African diaspora. The Anglophone Afro-Caribbean cultural praxis of Obeah
(aka Obi) can be traced historically through multidisciplinary analytic lens of
African hegemonic beliefs transported through the Transatlantic Middle passage to the diaspora. Obeah as an indigenous, religio-spiritual practice and set
of beliefs is squarely rooted in the African polytheistic traditions. Embracing

a complex history, Obeah influenced herbalism, mediumship, divination, and other metaphysical machinations engendering a plethora of representations. Although Bilby and Handler in their article, *Obeah: Healing and Protection in West Indian Slave Life*, state that "Obeah is not an organized religion," an issue contradicted, firstly, by their descriptions of the bifurcated and fundamental characteristics of the practice as controlling supernatural forces, and secondly, by divination which entails the following: protective rituals of healing, illness-diagnosis, and harm protection (Bilby and Handler 2004). It begs the question: How could Obeah then be represented as unorganized? The argument appears both impoverished and a non sequitur.

Barima asserts the claim of its coherence as a "religious cultural system inherited between generations" (Barima 2016, 16). Further, he adds, "with its own liturgy, spiritual hierarchy and herbal repository, Obeah clearly is more than a simple remnant of West and Central African religion" (Barima 2016, 24). Moving beyond this, is his central thesis that Obeah was weaponized in the antislavery, anti-colonial movement as a viable political and military contestation and threat to the oppressive and reprehensible slave system. Referring to the curative dimensionalities of Obeah, Barima states that

> [I]ts resources were heavily tapped to cure minor and extreme illnesses and Charles Walker, while explaining Obeah's medicinal benefits, described diverse herbs and their preparations. Addressing illnesses and knowing curative plants, barks, and roots were important in the Obeah man's trade. Healing, however, for the Obeah man was defined more broadly than correcting physical ailments. (Barima 2016, 22)

It entailed inducing good fortunes, providing spiritual protection, and assisting with pedantic, everyday concerns.

Like all things African, Obeah as viewed through the colonial gaze was rooted in the underground, subterranean bowels of Hades. Perennially represented as primordial, it was propagandized as wanton savagery. Representations of Obeah calcified the practices as emanating from a degenerate set of beliefs rooted in primitivism, sans a marginalized reference to the practitioner's goals to heal and cure. Despite persistent and full-throttled efforts to challenge its central authority in Maroon communities, legal and social efforts to subvert, criminalize, and stamp out its presence failed immeasurably. Anthropologists Bilby and Steady in their 1981 essay, "Black Women and Survival: A Maroon Case," identified Grandy Nanny as the revolutionary leader of the Windward Maroons of Jamaica. As a leader, she is revered and in possession of supernatural gifts. She is an Obeah-woman, a "science-woman whose mystical powers 'symbolizes the continuity of Maroon society through time and space.'" Interestingly, Nanny is described as a woman born in Africa from the *Akan* people. The Akan people from the Gold Coast were the primary Obeah practitioners in the Caribbean Basin.

Given that Yemonja, also called Yemaya or Iemanja is one of the premier deities of the Yoruba people, Nanny as mediator would have by all indices of cultural transmission known and embraced the Feminine Divine, the "Prime Mother of all things." It is conceivable that European understanding of Obeah as an anathematic counterforce to their colonial vice grip would not have recorded, accepted, or validated any explicit African deities or spiritualists, as their central core patriarchal ideology could not fathom the concept of a Feminine Divine. However, African belief systems embraced Yemonja in the pantheon of gods; she governed water, the source of life itself and the disproportionate composition of our corporal bodies.

However, Cliff in an article published inside the *Journal of Feminist Studies in Religion* describes Nanny as the "daughter of Yemaya" and that "God as 'her'-thrills and startles because we live in a culture that teaches above all that God is masculine" She adds, "[T]he female authority came with African men and women to the New World and the slave communities. It was embodied in Grandy Nanny" (1985, 11–13). It is the fact that Yemonja is the mother of all the Orishas makes the Feminine Divine normative in African theology, countering what Barima alliteratively calls "Christianity chauvinism." She is the linchpin to the Maroon community's survival as she plies her superiority in the supernatural arts.

In the narrative telling of the courageous stances of Nanny in the ultimate liberation and protection of her people, the fact that we lay claim and reclamation to her penultimate existence finds goodness-of-fit with the Afrocentric womanist epistemology which validates and affirms Black women's experiences (Hill 1990). Nanny's victories waged psychological violence on the colonial forces as her insurgency and military victories of resistance interrogated, contested, and inverted the fragile concept of white hegemonic power. Obeah practitioners were hunted down, prosecuted, and executed in attempts to abrogate their ability to traverse the spiritual to secular in their liberation struggles. Many of these Obeah practitioners combined Christian symbolism and mysticism to enhance their appeal. Healers wielded incalculable power.

In literary discourses, Obeah's salience has been magnified. Kenneth Bilby, an anthropologist and ethnomusicologist, found that there are mixed and contradictory representations of Obeah in cultural expressions and songs based on his ethnographic interviews in Maroon communities in Suriname, Jamaica, and French Guiana. Titling his publication in a nod to the iconic Bob Marley's song, *An (Un)natural Mystic in the Air: Images of Obeah in Caribbean Song,* his central thesis is that Obeah "remains a primary site of cultural contestation" because post-colonial, reductionistic representations of Obeah see this legacy of Africanism as evil, bad, and negative (Bilby 2012,

45–79). He generously provides the reader with lyrics of songs that vilify Obeah practitioners as evil, charlatans echoing the colonial legacy in post-colonial times. On the other hand, a number of reggae and Calypso artists are using the Obeah moniker as a kind of "unspoken cultural vindication—a gesture toward reclaiming ancestral power thorough music or other African-related forms of cultural expression, and in some cases an attempt to reas-sert control over the language used to characterize such ancestral power" (Bilby 2012, 49). Just to name a few, other literary works such as *Hammel, the Obeah Man*, Calypsonians such as the Mighty Sparrow's song *Melda, the Obeah Wedding* have fused in our cultural consciousness the continuity between past and the contemporary.

It is noteworthy that renowned Francophone Caribbean writers such as Maryse Conde have integrated issues of folk healing traditions as a prominent force in Afro-Caribbean literature and lionize the power of these beliefs as central to the narration. Although the work is fictional, and what Jane Moss in her 1999 article entitled *Postmodernizing the Salem Witchcraze: Maryse Conde's, I, Tituba, Black Witch of Salem* calls a "historiographic metafiction" because of its history-fictional literature fusion, the protagonist Tituba, an Amerindian slave woman from Barbados uses her curative powers to heal, communicate with the dead, and tell fortunes. The discourse surrounding autobiographical narration of a slave woman is considered a revengeful act against colonialism according to Angela Davis.

According to Moss, writing about Conde's motives that she

> wants Tituba to be a witch, but a witch in the Afro Caribbean sense of the word—a woman with knowledge of the natural world and spiritual links to the invisible world. She wants her to be guilty of doing harm to her evil enemies and challenging the authority of those who abuse her. And finally, she wants Tituba to subvert historical perspectives and cultural codes radically in order to re-invent herself in her own words. (Moss 1999, 15)

In an attempt to eschew what she describes as "the exoticization of Caribbean life," Paton states that, "Obeah was a *mutual* construction, made in the spaces between the powerful's imposition and the colonized's resis-tance; but also, and more importantly, moving beyond assumptions about the permanent division between the always-imposing colonizer and the always-resisting colonized." What she is referring to is the nature of acculturation which informs and shapes this cultural intersection. It is noteworthy that Paton states that "the recent decriminalization of Obeah in Anguilla (1980), Barbados (1998), Trinidad and Tobago (2000), and St Lucia (2004)" show how longstanding this preoccupation with Obeah has been even in the post-colonial Anglophone Caribbean. In 2013, the Governor General in Jamaica signed an *Obeah Amendment Act* to prohibit whippings as a penalty for "certain criminal offense."

Obeah practices involved using oils, herbs, and chemicals; work with talismans; incense; ancestral worship; massages; calling ancestors with incantations; using hair, skin, soap, clothing; and creating wooden effigies. The Obeah piccanini (wooden effigies) were conduits and custodians for the Orisha spirits. In addition, clays pots with water, kola nuts, and cowry shells were employed by diviners to facilitate spirit contact.

Wedenoja addressed Jamaican folk-healing traditions in a syncretic Afro-Christian religion called "Revival." He writes in a 1983 report that "Balmists combine African herbalism and divination with Christian beliefs." He views balm yards as an "institutionalized extension of motherhood" as they treat a plethora of pathologies: psychosomatic illnesses, pains in the body, high blood pressure, urinary disorders, gastro-intestinal distress, headaches, mental pathologies, and other malaises related to living. In extending the mother metaphor, it appears that the Feminine Divine was embraced and incorporated into patterns of healing and spirit restorations (Wedenoja 1983, 6).

The Yoruba people have had a rich history as one of African's largest population. As such, the role of religion and their belief systems permeated the fabric of their lives. Yemonja, Mother of all Orishas, is a venerated Yoruba Orisha. Goddess of fertility, she cares deeply for her children, provides comfort, and is a cleansing goddess. From her womb, creation emerged. She is the Mother of Water, deity of the Ogun River, depicted as a mermaid, and governs all activities related to women: conception, childbirth, healing, love, and safety. Her wealth is represented by cowrie shells, and although temperate, she is capable of unleashing destructive forces such as flood waters and turbulences in rivers, creeks, lagoons, streams, springs, and lakes. She has been syncretized with other religions such as Catholicism.

As is characteristic of all religious systems, there are sacred objects, ritual sacrifices, ritual foods, and festivals. Sacred objects associated with Yemonja in New World worship include the following: dishes and porcelain, earthen basins, fruits, white jars or pitchers, white medals, and coins. Ritual sacrifices depending on lineage include guinea fowl, ducks, and she-goats. Animal sacrifices were disposed of in the water, congruent with her being Mother of the Water. Rituals foods range from manioc or maize flour boiled in milk or water, corn meal, onions, rice, white corn, white corn meal boiled in coconut milk and the fruit, obi.

Given their involuntary removal from West Africa from where the Yoruba peoples came, this patron spirit of women owns rivers, streams, and oceans. People from Nigeria, Benin, Brazil, Cuba, and Uruguay are avid practitioners and devotees of Yemonja. There are a number of myths that show Yemonja in her fullness, including her marriage and motherhood. Many of them are unsubstantiated. In diametrical contrast, given how persecuted Obeah practices were under colonialism and post colonialism in the English-speaking Caribbean, overt venerations and open practices celebrating the connections to African deities were not permitted. Therefore, there is a research vacuum on the threadings of Yemonja and Obeah. One can examine the practices by assessing the underlying similarities through direct or oblique references. Since the Akan people from the Gold Coast were the primary Obeah practitioners in the Caribbean Basin, given that documented history, the notions of cleansing and consecrated baths fully consolidated and supported in Obeah practices as a modality for healing are congruent with the Orisha Yemonja connections with the aquatic world.

The role and symbolism of water in the Yemonja tradition warrants amplification. Water symbolizes cleansing, renewal, rebirth, protection, and purging. Enslaved people participating in the 1823 Boxing Day Revolt were bathed in water prepared by practitioners of Obeah. A noteworthy addition to the bath was sage, a bush designed to fortify one from spiritual weaknesses (Barima 2016). The use of sage though may have served a plethora of usages. Since it is a scented plant, its placement in water may have produced a therapeutic, uplifting, and olfactory-sensorial experience. However, *Salvia divinorum*, which was used by diviners—hence its name—is an herbal sage mint that has psychoactive properties and can induce hallucinations when chewed, smoked or consumed in a tea. Salvia white sage has been connected to enhanced cognition and more astute focus and also used by Obeah practitioners.

In conclusion, the preservation and rootedness of African belief systems in the Anglophone Caribbean could only occur because of the power of those traditions to be maintained and upheld by devotees willing to wage warfare. Obeah survived despite persistent efforts aimed at its eradication. In the end, Yemonja in her supreme role of mother, mothered her descendants, ensuring their ultimate survival and continuity.

REFERENCES

Barima, Kofi Boukman. 2016. "Cutting Across Space and Time: Obeah's Service to Jamaica's Freedom Struggle in Slavery and Emancipation." *Africology: The Journal of Pan African Studies* 9, no. 4 (July).

Bilby, Kenneth M., and Jerome S. Handler. 2004. "Obeah: Healing and Protection in West Indian Slave Life." *The Journal of Caribbean History* 38, no. 2 (2004).

———. 2012. "An (Un)Natural Mystic in the Air: Images of Obeah in Caribbean Song." *Obeah and Other Powers: The Politics of Caribbean Religion and Healing*, 45–79. https://doi.org/10.1215/9780822394839-002.

Cliff, Michelle. 1985. "I Found God in Myself and I Loved Her/I Loved Her Fiercely." *Critical Theory Women, Feminist Identity and Society in the 1980s*, 101. https://doi.org/10.1075/ct.1.10cli.

Collins, Patricia Hill. 1990. *Black Feminist Thought: Knowledge, Consciousness, and the Politics of Empowerment*. New York: Routledge, Taylor & Francis Group.

Condé Maryse. 2016. *I, Tituba, Black Witch of Salem*. Vancouver, BC: Langara College.

Davis, Angela. 2019. *Women, Race and Class*. New York: Penguin.

Moss, Jane. 1999. "Postmodernizing the Salem Witchcraze: Maryse Conde's I, Tituba, Black Witch of Salem." *Colby Quarterly* 35, no. 1 (1999).

Olmos Margarite Fernández, and Lizabeth Paravisini-Gebert. 2000. *Sacred Possessions: Vodou, Santería, Obeah, and the Caribbean*. New Brunswick, NJ: Rutgers University Press.

Olupona, Jacob. "The Spirituality of Africa." *The Harvard Gazette*. Interview with Anthony Chiorazzi. October 6, 2015. https://news.harvard.edu/gazette/story/2015/10/the-spirituality-of-africa/.

Paton, Diana. 2012. *Obeah and Other Powers: The Politics of Caribbean Religion and Healing*. Durham, NC: Duke University Press.

———. 2015. *The Cultural Politics of Obeah: Religion, Colonialism and Modernity in the Caribbean World*. Cambridge: Cambridge University Press.

Payne-Jackson, Arvilla. 2004. *Jamaican Folk Medicine: A Source of Healing*. Kingston: University Press of the West Indies.

William, Wedenoja. 1989. *Mothering and the Practice of "Balm" in Jamaica*. New Brunswick: Rutgers University Press.

Chapter 5

What Does It Mean to Be a Traditional Priestess?

Interrogating Women's Engagement with the Divine

Grace Sintim Adasi

INTRODUCTION

This essay looks at the lives of priestesses of African Tradition Religion (ATR) in Ghana. The diversity of religious movements in Africa, and in Ghana in particular, means that ATR co-exists with other religions, most notably Christianity and Islam, and also in more recent times, the proliferation of other Eastern-world religions such as Buddhism, Hinduism, and other traditions. While the co-existence of these belief systems has been generally peaceful, ATR and Christianity, especially Evangelical Christianity, have always had a negative relationship as a result of some Christians' perceptions of and attitudes toward ATR. The difficult relationship between ATR and Christianity was derived directly from the attitude of missionaries toward ATR. This attitude was further perpetuated by colonialists, anthropologists, and in recent dispensations, Evangelical Christians such as Pentecostals and Charismatics.

The history of the negative perceptions and treatment of ATR can be traced to colonialism and Western anthropologists' perception of casting African culture, and by extension, religion as the other and inferior to Western culture and religion. Fage, for instance, notes that during the early years of missionary activities, Africans were regarded as people without any history and as such could not have religion as well (cited in Sackey 2009). In furtherance of this agenda, any practices that seemed to have any connections with ATR was treated with contempt and reduced to objects of ridicule. To this end, ATR was described as "fetishism," "paganism," "heathenism," "animism," and other such derogatory terms. Such descriptions were surprisingly advanced by earlier African scholars who had yielded to the tenets of colonization and were highly disconnected to decipher the Western agenda to denigrate everything African.

Sackey 2009 cites Kingsley (1951, 32) as noting that "when I say juju or fetish, I mean the religion of the natives of West Africa." Sackey (2009), gives an example of a vice chancellor and an official of the Accra Metropolitan Assembly (the governing body of the Accra Metropolis, the capital of Ghana) as having used the term "fetish priest." The vice chancellor and the public official's blunders are quite disappointing since they epitomize the two institutions that are expected to be invested in the knowledge of African culture, and by extension, its religions. However, this also is a good starting point for one to understand the ways in which ATR is perceived and understood, packaged and presented to, and sometimes by, Africans themselves. It is such attitudes toward ATR that have emboldened some Pentecostal and Charismatic dispensations to make derogatory comments about and openly disrespect ATR. In one such occurrence, a prophet known as Adarkwa Yiadom threw an open challenge to a renowned priest, Nana Kwaku Bonsam, at the National Stadium. On the said date of the challenge a huge crowd came to witness this monumental incident, but only the priest turned up. Of course, the prophet earned public ridicule while this incident boosted the popularity of the priest (see https://www.peacefmonline.com/pages/local/religion/200805/33186.php). Indeed, another pastor has gained tremendous popularity and following because of his professed hatred for ATR worship. His very trade name is Osofo Kyiriabosm (The pastor who hates deities). His private television station (Fire TV) continuously broadcast his exploits of destroying artefacts, shrines that "housed" the gods, as well as visiting river sites to declare them powerless and rain insults on them. The rationale being that, if such river deities are powerful, then they should have retaliated in response to his insults. He has gained such a following that he has gone to the extent of forming a political party, known as the Ghana Unio n Movement (see https://www.modernghana.com/news/958822/sofo-kyiri -abosom-launches-ghana-union-movement.html). Ironically, while he claims to align his political ideas with Dr. Kwame Nkrumah, the first President of Ghana, his religious ideals are at par with that of Dr. Nkrumah, a fervent promoter of ATR.

I should note that the persistent attacks on ATR seem not to have successfully drowned the religion, at least in Ghana, as there has been the recent proliferation of adverts, billboards, and radio and television shows organized by some priests and priestesses. Indeed, some very popular ones own television stations where they advertise their services and sometimes showcase their exploits.

While ATR is practiced among all ethnic groups and people in Ghana, my focus in this chapter is on the Akan. While the Akan are not exceptionally peculiar in their practice of ATR, I am particularly interested in the priesthood among them because of the peculiar place of women in the Akan society. In the following discussion, I attend to the Akan worldview, and the place of women in the Akan society. I then discuss the Akan woman as a priestess and how she manages her calling and ordinary life. My data for the work consist of a focus group discussion with priestesses, interviews with some of the priestess and shrine attendants, and observations at three different shrines. The focus group discussion was initiated with five priestesses but later ended with six when another priestess walked in to greet and join the group. This group was the priestesses who had come to pay allegiance and join in the celebration at the Akonedi shrine. Issues raised and discussed in the focus group discussion included their calling, experiences, and difficulties, as well as the ways in which they balanced their lives. The interviews were held at the shrines of two priestesses and three other shrine attendants made up of three men and a woman. The larger part of the observations occurred at the Akonedi shrine (a renowned shrine in Ghana, located among the Larteh ethnic group), during the annual thanksgiving festival. On this occasion, I was privileged to be allowed to sit among priestesses as they conducted rituals and other activities such as going around the vicinity of the shrine, sprinkling ɛtɔ (mashed plantain with red palm oil, normally used as a food for ritual) at certain times. From this privileged position, I was able to observe as well as participate in mundane conversations with priestesses and other servants at the shrines. I observed priestesses tease one another about regular everyday issues such as aging, food, and relationships.

My entrance into the lives of these women was through an insider. However, my position as a reverend minister of the Presbyterian Church of Ghana was a significant factor in being accepted and establishing a relationship with the women. My interest in and focus on the priesthood was also a source of curiosity to the priestesses who questioned the cause of my interest. In an interaction, I was able to convey my other position as an academic and a researcher and my fascination with women's encounters with the divine. I further intimated that my interest even in this area of research was also a direct result of my personal experience of being called to serve as a priest. Finally, another point of convenience was the fact that I came from the Presbyterian Church. Almost all the priestesses shared that while they were subjected to attack and abuse by some Christian practitioners, they were also on good terms with others. They cited the Presbyterian and Methodist churches as among those with whom they had cordial relationships. Indeed, they noted that their relationship with what I cautiously called the mainline Protestant congregations (Presbyterian, Anglican, Methodist, Baptist) was mostly one of tolerance, accommodation, respect and friendliness toward each other. There is no easy way to "enter" the intimate spaces of others; however, in this instance, my position as a priest and woman was my converging point with these women.

The Akan Worldview

The Akan are the largest ethnic group in Ghana, which comprises the Bono, Asante, Kwahu, Akyem, Fante, Akuapem, Akuamu, Denkyira, Wassa, and the Sefwi (Agyekum 2018). The Akan are bound together and identified as one group because of their linguistic and cultural similarities with little variations in few instances. The one practice that sets the Akan out of other ethnic groups in Ghana is their inheritance arrangement. The line of descent, which also informs the identity and rights of inheritance of every individual in Akan, is matrilineal. This means that any child born into the Akan community belongs to the mother's family and, therefore, acquires property through the mother's line, mostly from the mother's brother(s). This does not imply that fathers do not play a role in the child's life (Assimeng 1989). Indeed, while the child inherits the mother's *mogya* (blood), it is believed that it is the father who gives the child his *kra* (Soul). It is, therefore, the father who names the child and is primarily responsible for the financial upkeep, disciplining and training of children. However, the fact that a woman and her children belong to her lineage places women in a very crucial position in Akan society. For without a woman, the lineage will cease to exist. This means that Akan women occupy a peculiar privileged position and can access as well as use family lands and other related resources. This also strengthens women's positions, especially in marriage. Just like their husbands, women can move about freely, join associations of their choice, and engage in economic ventures without the express permission of their husbands. Women are not obliged to keep the universal economic purse with their husbands, and a woman who feels her interests are not being met in a marriage can initiate and get a divorce (Abu 1983). This position of an Akan woman applies in almost all circumstances, even if she is called by the deity as a priestess.

The Akan cosmopolitan is not peculiarly unique in comparison to other Africans. As is mostly the case, there is first and foremost the belief in the Supreme Being, known as Nyame or Onyankopon through whom all things live and obtain their existence. All forms of worship is ultimately directed to Nyame. As has been noted by Kofi Asare Opoku, all the names and attributes of God in almost all African societies "express the idea of uniqueness of God" (1978, 14). In the Akan understanding, Nyame is perceived as possessing both male and female characteristics, hence the appellation Obaatanpa Nyankopon (the good mother God). This conception runs through most

African religious practices, for instance, among the Ga of Ghana, God is called Ataa Naa Nyonmo (Grandfather, Grandmother, God).

This dual conception of God in most African cosmology is significant for the recognition of the African feminine divine. This is extended to his representatives on earth, so that spirits in the form of deities can either be male or female. Next after the Nyame are the Abosom. Abosom are the spiritual representatives of Nyankopon and can inhabit both space and objects. According to Badejo (1998), they are associated with nature, and more specifically with rivers.

The presence and belief in Abosom have been one of the contested and most misrepresented aspects of ATR. Earlier anthropologists and Westerners argued that Africans, and in this case Akans, could not have religion because they believed in manmade or inanimate objects (Opoku 1978). Indeed, the very word, "paganism," used to describe the belief and practices of Africans points to this argument. It is, however, obvious that these foreigners, who neither understood the language nor culture of Africans, missed the point. The objects themselves are not the points of veneration but the spirits that inhabit the objects that are worshipped. Indeed, the objects are useless until the spirits are summoned through libation, invocation, and sometimes singing and dancing (Nrenzah 2005). In the words of Nevadomsky and Rosen, in ATR "the power is not in the objects themselves but in the person who has the spiritual ability" (1998, 207). The belief is therefore not in the objects, but the spirits that inhabit the objects and possess a human being. Indeed, the deities themselves are not deemed as infinitely powerful as God is, as a deity who refuses to respond to the supplications of supplicants can be abandoned or even earn scorn among the people (Opoku 1978). The human whom the gods possess happens to be one of the most significant parts of the story. They are known as Akomfo, and in Akan both men and women can be Akomfo. In his book, *Priesthood in Context*: Ekem notes that priesthood is

> a solemn vocation center on the choice of the *abosom* themselves regarding who should become their priests and priestesses. For this reason, a person cannot independently work his or her way into the priesthood and expect to be accorded the recognition and honor due to priests and priestesses. (2009, 48)

The Abosom are always the initiators in selecting the vehicles through which they want to manifest. As Ekem indicates, no one can become an Okomfo without the express possession by the spirit of a deity. Indeed, anyone who fakes a possession can count on a terrible or embarrassing verdict from a deity. The story is told of a young man who faked possession after his father's death. The father of this young man had been the Okomfo Panyin, and this young man who used to assist his father was confident that he was the obvious choice for the office of priesthood. From the knowledge gathered as a longtime assistant to his father, he started gathering herbs and prescribing healing for supplicants. He constantly faked spells of possession for quite some time. This charade, however, ended in embarrassment when the deity possessed the ten-year-old half-brother of this older son, as the selected Okomfo for the town. The deity showed that indeed it was the final decider for the person that carried out its will (Personal communication with Eunice Kwao, a key informant).

The selection of a person as a priest is significant since they act as the representative and vehicle through whom the will of the deity is known to the people, and the supplications of the people are carried to the deity (Rosenthal 1998). The primary role of a priest or priestess is to serve as an intermediary between humans and the deity; in other jurisdictions, they also serve as political heads, judges, and ritual experts (13–14). These roles are very important in the African society, as a new chief is expected to work closely with the Omanhene (king) to avert crises such as sudden and recurrent death in a town and the outbreak of epidemics. Again, they serve as judges who settle both spiritual and physical grievances. In cases such as accusations of witchcraft and theft, the Okomfo can quickly be summoned to the chief's palace or his elders sent to the shrine to ascertain the truth. They also conduct rituals to avert deaths and calamities in instances where there has been *duabo* (ritual curses).

The health-providing roles of the Okomfo makes them one of the most sought-after health providers in Ghana. Health in Africa in general and Akan in particular is a holistic experience, entailing physical, mental, and spiritual well-being. Badejo has noted that "the priestesses who train in their respective traditions are also herbalists and traditional doctors" (Badejo 1998, 99). They provide a whole range of health services for both men and women. The Okomfo can be consulted on issues such as infertility, madness, wealth, etc. The Okomfo is thus "at once a friend, priestess, doctor, social worker, advisory bureau, psychologist, psychiatrist and philanthropist" (Appia-Kubi, cited in Sackey 2009, 187).

It is of great importance that Sackey notes that although the office of the priesthood is open to men and women, there tend to be more priestesses than priests among the Akans (Sackey 1989, 2009). This is strictly different from Western religions such as Christianity, which until recently, did not open its priesthood doors to women. The fact that one of the highest offices in Akan society is open to women is a further reflection of the special position women hold in the society. Badejo, for instance, notes that "the chief priestess in the Akan structure also provides some examples of mythico-religious foundations of power and femininity in African social order" (1998, 99). Feminine power, whether secular or divine has been and continues to be a potent force to be reckoned with in almost all African societies. Most deities in Akan and in most African societies are female. The legend of Mami Wata, for instance, occupies a central theme in feminine sacred power in most West African Religious. Mami Wata has been described as a "sacralization of the feminine within Igbo culture and tradition" (4). Yemoja, considered an Orisa is also the mother of all Orisa. She is a goddess of water and the giver of children (Opoku 1978, 65). Her name, which means "Mother Whose Children Are the Fishes," is an affirmation of her ability to produce an endless number of children to supplicants, as her children are "as uncountable as the fish in the sea" (Juju 2019). The powers of Yemoja and her adherents are not restricted to Yoruba land, as she is worshipped in Brazil as a sea goddess and in other places such as Cuba and Argentina, with name variations such as Yemaja and Yemanja (Juju 2019). Thus, Yemoja is recognized as an international deity, carried over through the Transatlantic Slave Trade.

As has been noted, the priesthood in Akan has more females than men. This is also as a result of the fact that most of these deities are water deities who are associated with fertility and reproduction. Another probable explanation for this occurrence is the concept of marriage between the deity and the priestess. The metaphor of marriage is extended to describe the relationship between these male deities and the female priestess, "w'aware no" (the deity has married her). For instance most of the priestesses interviewed for this study were priestesses to deities such as Adade Kofi, Asuo Gyebi, and Asi Ketewa (all male deities and associate deities of the Larteh) and described their relationship as being in a marital union with the deity, "wa ware me" (the deity has married me). This does not, however, include a sexual union between the two, but a working relationship that is so intimate that it can only be explained in those terms.

The worship and veneration of deities, mostly water deities which are feminine, is as a result of their association with fertility. This association with procreation creation creates an innumerable number of devotees for these deities. The reverence accorded to these deities is transferred and reflected in the ways in which their priestesses are feared and respected. In the narrations below, I use the abbreviations "P" to mean Priestess and serial numbers (e.g., 1, 2, etc.) to represent my study participants.

The Call to Serve

As with most documented calls to the priesthood (Sackey 2009), some of these priestesses' calls were met with suspicion and rejection. Two of the priestesses narrate their experiences:

> When we found out what it was, I didn't want it and neither did my family and this led to my going in and out of coma. I was taken to Father Cashmiere's

(the Catholic priest at post) place, but he couldn't help. We are Christians you see. We went to so many pastors, even Christo Asafo (a renowned Christian congregation in Ghana) but all to no avail. Eventually, my parents consulted Nana Sewaa at Tweapease who brought me to Larteh (a renowned shrine) to train. (P.1)

I was in Primary 2 when it started. My father refused to accept it. One day I got possessed throughout the day and the night and my father continuously hit my head with a Bible throughout the night. Eventually, he took me to my uncle's house (mother's brother) and had me locked up upstairs while they met down-stairs to discuss what to do. When they later came to check on me, I had disap-peared downstairs waiting for them. That was when they realized that they could really do nothing about this and started consulting shrines to find answers. (P.2)

The refusal of both the priestess and the family to allow their child to serve is a recurrent theme in the lives of most priestess. The rejection could be a collective decision from the family or from the person who has received the call. As has been noted by Sackey (2009), mostly, such refusals are as a result of the fact that both families and the person called are mostly Christians and therefore find it difficult to reconcile their beliefs with having a priestess in the family. However, in the instance of one of the participants, the reasons for rejection by the family was also as a result of the cost involved in the training of a neophyte. The process of undergoing training and graduation to become a full-fledged priestess involves a series of sacrifices, the acquisition of cer-tain items, as well as maintenance of the neophyte during training. It mostly lasts for three years. This can be quite expensive for most families and can be considered an unwelcome financial burden, especially by those families who are already unwilling to initiate their daughters.

Not all the calls were rejected; indeed, in one instance it was a welcome intervention. In the case of one of the priestesses, her call was the source of salvation from incessant death in her family. The priestess noted that she first got possessed as a young woman operating a "chop bar" (restaurant that serves local food). Initially, it was ignored with the hope that it would cease. Recurrent bouts of possession however prompted the family to consult a local shrine. Her possession also coincided with successive deaths of family members, which was still a mystery to the family. It took the family's con-sultation to ascertain the reason for her possession to find that the cause for the recurrent deaths was *duabo* (curses). The uncle (mother's brother) of the possessed girl had committed an offence for which he had been cursed by the offended party with the Larteh deity. It was further explained that when the deity visited the family to strike its next victim, the deity saw the beautiful young woman and fell in love with her. The deity had therefore decided to marry her. This was readily accepted by the family since it served to release them family from incessant deaths. In her own words: "Nobody resisted my call. In fact old men in my family were the ones who brought me to Larteh to be trained. When it was time for my graduation, it was no joke at all. They went all out to ensure a beautiful ceremony and to establish me as a priestess" (P. 3).

While it could be said that she atoned for the sins of another family member, the priestess in this particular story did not express any bitterness on this score, rather, she saw her call as a privilege to be the one chosen to save her family. However, it must be said that not all priestesses are amenable to playing the "sacrificial role." A key informant narrated the sad case of a young woman in her hometown whose call to the priesthood had taken the same route as that of P.3 narrated above. She, too, had been possessed by a deity that had visited her family to kill a member due to a *duabo* and had decided to marry the beautiful young girl. She was therefore pulled out of school and trained as a priestess. According to my informant, this situation did not sit well with the priestess who could experience the onslaught of intense anger and frustration at her situation. In one such instance she is noted to have pronounced:

> When you (family members) go around misbehaving, then it's me the innocent one who must atone for your nonsense. Don't I, a beautiful young woman deserve better? Don't I deserve to have completed my education and have a decent job in a decent office? Yet, I have been reduced to serving as a priestess for a crime I did not commit while my colleagues work in an office as I would have loved to do. The most annoying part of all this is that I was not the one who committed the crime. (Personal communication with Eunice Kwao, key informant)

This young priestess in question never fully accepted her call although she was trained, graduated and worked as a priestess. She is reported to have continuously flouted the rules and taboos of the deity, an action which eventually led the deity to kill her (this was revealed when her family consulted another deity after what they considered to be her untimely death).

Whether they accept or have reservations about the call, none of the priestesses have control in the decision to serve or do otherwise. Indeed, as already indicated above, the individual who is chosen to serve is the sole prerogative of the deity. The story of these two women is significant in the discussion of how priestesses make sense of their world and their call to serve the divine.

The incessant attacks by evangelical Christianity on ATR (Owusu-Ansah 2017) could lead a believer or practitioner of ATR to doubt their future especially in stances where Christianity, the most dominant religion in the country, has drawn the conclusion that anyone who believes in other gods is bound for the Christian hell. However, none of the priestesses in this study indicated any regrets or fears for their spiritual future. Indeed, they discussed their call and their work with the clear conviction that they have been equally called by God. One priestess indicated as such:

> The truth is that we got possessed while sitting in the church. We did everything in the beginning to end this but all our efforts were to no avail. In my case I kept going in and out of coma. And this makes you then begin to reason that God has equally called you. If we stop now we could die or something terrible could happen. I believe I am doing God's work through this possession. If someone is planning evil destruction or death against another person and I am able to foul that plan then I believe I have done God's work. We are on this earth and know that there are malevolent spirits but we don't know what is in heaven. This is how we are also doing God's work on earth. (P.1)

> We were all sitting in church when this call came. We did everything to stop it in the beginning because we were afraid because you are told that worshiping a deity is evil. We visited pastors, Catholic priests, all to no avail. I was sick for a long time because of this refusal. What you do also help people so how do you then call it evil? We don't do anything to hurt anyone, on the contrary we foul evil deeds, we heal, we help people to have children and to thrive an all that. How anyone can convince themselves that what we do here is evil, we leave those accusations to God. In the end, we will all find out. (P. 3)

Priestesses rationalize their call as a divine enterprise involving God and the abandonment or refusal to serve to have dire consequences. Indeed, the various afflictions which they had suffered at the initial stages of their call because of their refusal to serve are clear manifestation that abandonment at any point in the calling and service could incur the wrath and punishment from the deity. This understanding is similar to the Christian belief in a call to serve and the admonishment thereof of the consequences of those who refuse to serve or withdraw from the "plough" (Luke 9:57–62).

Extraordinary Women in Ordinary Lives

One of the most striking chapters in Chinua Achebe's *Things Fall Apart* is Chapter 6 in which Chielo, the priestess of Agbala, came to Okonkwo's house at night to take Ezinma to the shrine as had been decreed by the gods. In the deep of the night, the shrill voice of Chielo pierces the night. This is not a new occurrence; what is new this particular night is that the greetings are directed to the protagonist Okwonkwo's house. His favorite daughter Ezinma by his favorite wife Ekwefi was to be taken to the shrine of Agbala, as the deity had requested. Overcome by apprehension, Okwonkwo tries to plead on behalf of his recently ill daughter. The possessed priestess' response is a sudden scream and reprimand: "Beware, Okwonkwo! She warned. Beware of exchanging words with Agbala. Does a man speak when a god speaks? Beware!" (Achebe 1958, 89).

Okwonkwo fails at the negotiation and Ezinma is taken away. Ezinma, the little girl in question begins to cry because we are told "she was used to Chielo calling her my daughter. But it was a different Chielo she now saw in the yellow half-light" (1958, 80). Ezinma's cries also falls on deaf ears and she is whisked away by the priestess. The fear of the unknown befalling her child who had just been carried away by the possessed priestess causes Ekwefi to dash after the priestess. However, the pitch dark night becomes unbearably frightening for the troubled mother who at one point decides to call the priestess for companionship. But Ekwefi suddenly realizes that "It was not the same Chielo who sat with her in the market and sometimes bought bean-cakes for Ezinma, who she called her daughter. It was a different woman, the priestess of Agbala, the oracles of the Hills and Caves" (1958, 80).

I use Achebe's eloquent depiction of the priestess as an entry point in discussing the lives of the priestesses in my study because there is surprisingly no difference between any of these women and Agbala. While their constant encounters with the divine transforms them into extraordinary positions, the priestesses who were engaged in the present study, are seemingly ordinary women who live ordinary lives and engage in equally mundane day-to-day activities like any other women.

Marriage is acceptable among the priestess and this could be arranged with any man the priestess fancies although such a selection must be approved by the deity. The justification given for the need for a deity approval was that during the call and throughout her life, a priestess is considered to be in both a familial and a marital relationship. The priestess is said to be married to the deity but at the same time considered a child of the deity. As one priestess describes it:

> You are at once the wife and child of the deity. You are the wife, pardon me to say not in the sexual sense of the word, but because you are the medium, the vehicle through which they are manifested. Also, because you are an automatic worshipper of the deity, you come under its protection so you are a child of the deity. A man who wants to marry you must therefore understand that he is taking into marriage both a wife and child of the deity and must thus pay compensation. (P. 5)

This requires that the man who marries a priestess must perform the marriage rites twice; one for her family of procreation and the other for the deity.

A man who was married before her calling is, however, not required to fulfill such requirements but is expected to fully assist and support his wife through her training and practice. While some of the priestesses in the study were married, others were divorced. Those who were married indicated that they led married lives like other non-possessed women and performed the duties expected of married women in their society. However, a married priestess is required to undergo spiritual cleansing after sex before attending to the deity. There are also purification rituals performed for a priestess three months after delivery before she can enter the presence of the deity. The specifics of the requirements for a ritual vary from deity to deity but the essence of such rites is that they are always geared toward the purification and sanctification of the priestess before she is able to serve again. The divorced priestesses indicated that their divorces had no connection with their position as priestess. It was stressed that despite their position as priestess they also encountered marital problems such as unfaithful and exploitative husbands. However, their final decision and position to leave the marriage had been strengthened by the belief and reliance on the support of the deity they serve. As one priestess noted:

> It is painful to be cheated by a man and even as priestess, we suffer the same. The only difference in our case is that you will know because sometimes the deity will alert you. In some cases, the deity will warn the man to desist or suffer the consequences and some husbands will heed the warnings but others will not. When the behaviour persists, you the woman realise that the deity might even kill the man so in this case you leave the marriage. Even if the deity does not intend to harm the man, it is annoying and quite upsetting to stay with a man like that. This is because what the deity can provide for me, in-term of economic sustenance and protection, you the man cannot. So why stay in such a marriage then? (P.2)

There is enough literature to indicate that most women enter into marriage due to the economic support and general protection expected to be provided by men (Adomako Ampofo 2000). When such expectations are not met or can be acquired from other places, it weakens the marital bond. For instance, it is well noted among the Akan that the strong ties to one's matrilineage and the expectation of support from the extended family dwindles reliance on one's spouses and places more allegiance and affinity with the family than spouses (Abu 1983). In the case of the priestesses, the reliance on the deity for whatever they believe would have benefited from the marriage becomes their insurance for leaving the marriage. While the priestesses at the time of the study held no form of employment some kept farms and had previous employments such as traders. Thus, they were depending solely on the charges and gifts they received from shrines, as well as remittances from older children.

Motherhood is a responsibility that priestesses embrace and aspire to. All the priestess in my interview sessions and focus group discussions had children and had good relationship with them. As one of them shared:

> The deities we serve love people; they also want people who will serve them so they make sure we have successful pregnancies and safe deliveries. If a priestess dies out of childbirth related issues then it is a punishment from the deity. In fact, you can be pregnant and be possessed. My best possession moments were when I was in labour because I don't feel the pains. By the time the possession is over you are almost close to pushing (Laughs). Our children also love and understand what they are born into. A child who disregards or is embarrassed by the mother does so because that child is just a bad one, not because the mother is a priestess. (P.5)

Indeed, during one of the visits with the research team, older children of one of the priestesses, together with their wives, husbands, and children had joined their mother to celebrate her annual thanksgiving celebration. A conversation with them revealed that they were all Christians; yet, they firmly believed in their mother's work as divinely ordained by God and were in full support of it. They visited and even sometimes asked for divine assistance and protection from the deity through their mother.

The position of priestess is seen as a process by the women involved in the study. The priestesses had responsibilities as mothers, nurturing their children and being actively involved in their upbringing. Unlike their male counterparts, these women have to balance their domestic responsibilities and their call to serve the divine. This is reminiscent of the experiences of women pastors who also have to combine their calling as pastors and their responsibilities as wives, mothers who also hold secular jobs (Adasi 2016). Despite these seemingly impossible expectations, they feel emboldened to undertake these activities because of their strong conviction of having the divine support of their deity and by extension that of God. The call to serve as a priestess was not a source of identity conflict or bifurcation for these women who throughout the research process were convinced of their calling and profession as an equally important act of salvation toward humanity. Attacks from evangelical Christianity was mainly perceived as failed attempts by pastors to convince congregants from patronizing the services of deities and ATR in general. The frustration that ATR continues to be a competitor in the religious landscape in Ghana has always been a sour point for most if not all Evangelical Christians, especially the pastors. Denigration of the deities, which translates into direct insults and abuses on priests and priestess, continues to be a common reaction from such pastors. Some priestesses narrated personal encounters with some so-called men of God who deem themselves as having been called to convert an idolatrous generation through preaching of the word, casting of demons, and a relentless attack on priests and priestesses and supplicants of deities. In one such remarkable encounter, the relationship between the priestess and the pastor had evolved from attack from the pastor to reconciliation and lasting friendship. The priestess narrates how this significant relationship transpired.

> Let me interrupt and tell you something about the phone call I just received. The caller was a pastor. He once visited my town for a crusade, and the deities and I became the butt of all his jokes and attacks. Some of my adherents came reporting it to me but I told them the gods can do their own battle. About two months later, I was at the shrine when they brought this man with swollen face, especially the mouth. It was such a sight. Apparently, he has been suffering the affliction right after his crusade. After various consultations it was revealed that he was being punished for his insults. We performed the rites and a day later he was healed. This is how we became friends and started teaching each other. Sometimes he sends me money, and anytime he has a program, he calls me for blessings like he just did. It is possible for us to live in harmony but they prefer to attack us. (P.3)

However, the response to such attacks also has a gendered angle. In recent times, Ghana has witnessed priests who have not only verbally responded to these assaults but have in some cases challenged such pastors into a show of spiritual prowess as was indicated above. While there have been threats from a renowned female priestess (the priestess of Akonedi) to pastors to err on the side of caution, these are few and far between and do not involve the fervor and call to challenge as the male priests do. Indeed, as was indicated by the priestesses, the responses and revenge are left in the hands of the gods, who are able to rise up to the occasion in defending and proving themselves powerful.

CONCLUSION

Priestesses are women who occupy the thin line between the physical and the spiritual worlds. The phenomenon of possession transforms ordinary women into vehicles through which the wills of deities are made manifest. While they are subject to the whims and caprice of the deities they serve, the deities also become a source of power for these women and this emboldens them to live ordinary lives and extraordinary circumstances. The priestesses are not immune to mundane experiences such as love, marriage, childbirth, and the demands and expectations of being a wife and a mother, nor are they insulated against life's exigencies such as divorce and the death of loved ones. A call to the priesthood has always been understood as the opportunity to serve at a higher office. When asked about how they reconcile their calling and their lives, priestesses indicated the seamless transition from their 'work' to their personal lives. First and foremost, they deem themselves as humans and women before priestesses. They revealed that it was their humanness that caused them to experience regular human emotions such as anger, love, happiness, sadness, and so on. Indeed, they also suffer losses, such as the untimely death of loved ones as well as divorce. It was indicated that their position as women in the society also led them to foster intimate relationships with men with the aim of marriage and procreation. One striking observation was the persistent wish by these women to be recognized as ordinary women who led everyday lives. The conviction was that the image of ATR that had been created by pastors tended to cast priestesses in an antagonistic position that leads some sections of society to perceive them with fear and suspicion. The aversion toward ATR and its adherents by some evangelical pastors and congregants means that priestesses are constantly at the receiving end of unprovoked attacks. While this is an attack on ATR in general, it is also an attack on the one space where women continue to hold very significant and powerful positions. Priestesses are, however, resilient and unperturbed by their challenges or attacks because of their strong conviction of being called by the God to fulfill a divine assignment. The belief in their encounter with the divine serves as a coping mechanism and the source of strength to live their extraordinary lives in ordinary ways.

REFERENCES

Abu, Kathrine. 1983. "The Separateness of Spouses: Conjugal Resources in an Ashanti Town." In *Female and Male in West Africa*, edited by Christine Oppong. London: George Allen & Unwin Pub. Ltd., 156–168.

Achebe, Chinua. 1958. *Things Fall Apart.* Oxford: Heinemann Educational Publishers.

Adasi, Grace Sintim. 2016. *Gender and Change: Roles and Challenges of Ordained Women Ministers of the Presbyterian Church of Ghana.* Accra: Gavoss Education PLC, Ltd.

Adomako Ampofo, Akosua. 2000. "Structural Inequalities or Gender Orientation, Which Matters More in Reproductive Decision Making? A Study Among Urban Ghanaian Couples." PhD diss., Vanderbilt University.Agyekum, Kofi. 2018. *Akan Body Parts Expressions: Cognitive Semantics and Pragmatic Approach.* Accra: Adwinsa Publications (GH) Ltd.

Assimeng, Max. 1989. *Religion and Social Change in West Africa.* Accra: Ghana University Press.

Badejo, Diedre L. 1998. "African Feminism: Mythical and Social Power of Women of African Descent." *Research in African Literatures* Vol 29, no. 2 (Summer): 94–111.

Boddy, Janice. 1994. "Spirit Possession Revisited: Beyond Instrumentality." *Annual Review of Anthropology* Vol 23 (October): 407–434.

Ekem, John David Kwamena. 2009. *Priesthood in Context: A Study of Priesthood in Some Christian and Primal Communities of Ghana and Its Relevance for Mother-Tongue Biblical Interpretation.* Accra: Sonlife Press.

Juju. "The Divine Feminine." https://medium.com/@emailthisjuju/the-divine-feminine-85b8c8488f14.

Madhu, K. 2012. "Mami Wata and the Occluded Feminine in Anglophone Nigerian-Igbo Literature." *Research in African Literatures* Vol 43, no. 1 (Spring): 1–18.

Nevadomsky, J., and Norma Rosen. 1988. "The Initiation of a Priestess: Performance and Imagery in Olukun Ritual." *TDR* Vol 32, no. 2 (Summer): 186–207. Accessed from https://www.jstor.org/stable/1145858.

Nrenzah, Genevieve. 2005. "Modernizing Indigenous Priesthood and Revitalizing Old Shrines: Current Development on Ghana's Religious Landscape." PhD diss., University of Bayreuth.

Opoku, Kofi. 1978. *West African Traditional Religion.* Jurong: FEP International Private Ltd.

Rosenthal, Judy.1998. *Possession, Ecstasy and Law in Ewe Voodoo.* Charlottesville and London: The University Press of Virginia.

Sackey, Brigid. 1989. "Aspects of Continuity in the Religious Roles of Women in 'Spiritual Churches' of Ghana." *Research Review* Vol 5, no. 2: 18–33.

———. 2009. "Power and Protest: Priesthood Among the Fante-Akan." *Research Review of African Studies Supplement 19. Knowledge Transmission in Ghana*: 179–197.

Part II

YEMONJA

LITERATURE, MEDIA, FILM

Chapter 6

Yemonja/Yemoja/Yemaya Rising

The Feminine Divine in Music, Fiction, and Media

Sheila Smith McKoy

For the cultures and the peoples of the African Diaspora, the most tell-ing inheritances of the *Maafa* are the ways that Diasporans use to access African spiritual practices. The trauma of the *Maafa*—as is true of all multi-generational, ancestral traumas—simultaneously created connection and disconnection because most Diasporans will never be able to identify their "original" points of origin (Richards 1981, 257). Many Diasporans, however, make this connection by embracing African-based spiritual practices. As an academic and a lover of African epistemologies, I have long been concerned with the *Maafa*, and the alien belief systems that were hierarchized—and often violently so—above African spiritual practices. Since human life began in Africa, it is worth noting that the deities in African belief systems existed long before the existence of Christianity, Islam, or Judaism from the "West," Confucianism, Taoism, Hinduism from the "East," or the spiritual traditions of the Americas before contact with Europeans. It is also interesting that one of the reasons European colonizers used to discredit the orisha was that they had human lives before ascending to the status of deities; those familiar with Christianity cannot escape the irony of this denigration. We must remember that colonization, enslavement, and conquering cultures not only disrupted the practice of African spiritualties but also attempted to erase the rever-ence for the African Feminine Divine. The energies associated with African female deities, then, were part of the first causalities of the European colo-nization and occupation of Africa. I add that African-based belief systems survived, despite the countless cultural, individual, spiritual, and spatial attempts to erase it.

That noted, there are millions of African Diasporans who continue to practice African spiritual practices. The embrace of and reclamation of the importance of the African Feminine Divine has also persisted in African and African descent cultures, despite the attempts at erasure. Perhaps the most well-known of these adherents is Zora Neale Hurston who, as a writer, anthropologist, and adherent of African-centered spiritual practices as a Voodoo priestess, describes this necessary work in *Dust Tracks on the Road* (1942). In this account, Hurston celebrates her connection to the African Feminine Divine:

> I have given myself the pleasure of sunrises blooming out of oceans, and sunset drenching heaped-up clouds. I have walked in storms with a crown of clouds about my head and the zigzag lightening playing through my fingers. The gods of the upper air have uncovered their faces to my eyes. I have found out that my real home is in the water, that the earth is only my step-mother. My old man, the Sun, sired me out of the sea . . . I know that destruction and construction are but two faces of Dame Nature, and that is it nothing to her if I choose to make a personal tragedy out of her unbreakable laws. (347–348)

In addition to inviting her readers to embrace spiritual practices beyond those left by the legacies of the *Maafa*, Hurston is one of several spiritual connectors to Yemonja, whom she clearly evokes in her reference to her home "in the water." Here, Hurston acknowledges the deeply rooted African-based traditions of Voodoo, Voodun, Hoodoo, and "roots" that have been practiced covertly and overtly since the arrival of Africans in the Americas.

This project focuses on the reclamation of the African Feminine Divine in acknowledgments to Yemonja in African Diasporan music, fiction, and media. Yemonja—once reclaimed—facilitates cultural survival and the formation of African-centric identity. Yemonja has a significant migratory history as a deity. Like the waters that she rules, the spiritual resonance of Yemonja extends far beyond Nigeria throughout the African Diaspora. Yemonja— whose domain includes the rivers, the most senior of all river deities—is positioned as the protector of the people who traversed the Atlantic during the *Maafa*. Here, it is useful to note that Yemonja's protection is credited with enabling the physical, psychic, and spiritual survivals of the people who came to the Americas and beyond in chains. In particular, I am interested in the ways that Yemonja is reclaimed in African Diasporan, especially African American, creative production from the period of enslavement to the present. In this project, I consider this vast and varied history by focusing on moments of movement back to the African Feminine Divine in general, and to Yemonja specifically. Her energy refuses to be bound by the dislocations experienced by the peoples and cultures of the African Diaspora. The immensity of

Yemonja's presence, then, cannot be denied. For this project, I refer to the recognition of her presence as Yemonja awakenings. However, because of the dislocations of the *Maafa*, I recognize three stages of enlightenment that lead to Yemonja awakenings in African Americans: the recognition of the spiritual realm, the recognition of ancestors, and the ritual processes that relate to African epistemological practices. Beyond these stages of enlightenment, I explore specific Yemonja awakenings that define the specific movements toward the embrace of Yemonja in music, literature, and film and the healing cultural work that they accomplish. While I certainly acknowledge that there are numerous examples of these awakenings, here, I focus on the musical collaboration of jazz pianist and composer Randy Weston, Melba Liston, and Langston Hughes in *Uhuru Africa*, which was released in 1960; the literary "conversation" between Octavia Butler's *Wild Seed* (1980) and the novel of her artistic progeny, Tomi Adeyemi, *Children of Blood and Bone* (2018); and Spike Lee's television series, *She's Gotta Have It* (2017 and 2019).

One of the mechanisms used to denigrate the African Feminine Divine is Western impulse to demonize the existence of spirits outside of those recognized by Christianity. In African Diasporan cultures, there have been numerous movements to recognize and celebrate the spiritual. One of the most important and understudied moments of this kind of awakening is associated with the nineteenth-century Spiritualist Movement. While we know many of the adherent's names, they are not usually associated with this movement which was defined by séances, mediumship, and table-knocking. The visionary, Sojourner Truth, who lived in a Spiritualist community in Battle Creek, Michigan, was well-known in this movement. Harriet Jacobs, author of *Incidents in the Life of a Slave Girl* (1861) also had a connection with the Spiritualist Movement, as did her editor, Lydia Maria Child. The most powerful connection of the early writers with the ancestral spiritual presence for me, however, is Harriet Wilson, author of *Our Nig: Sketches from the Life of a Free Black* (1859) whose autobiographical novel begins with a retelling of the events that led to her being abandoned as a young child and left with a family whose matriarch came from a slave-holding family in the South. Most editions of the book point to the fact that her life was tragic, in that she wrote the book to assist in the medical care of her son, who did not survive. She had a successful life after the publication of *Our Nig*, however. Wilson worked as a medium and was active in the Spiritualist Movement where she was recognized for her work with "spirit." While my research on her life is ongoing, Wilson and her contemporaries ushered in an acknowledged world of spiritual workings that overcame the illusions of race and white supremacy during an era defined by mastery and enslavement. These are only a few of the numerous movements to recognize "spirit" outside of Christianity in Diasporan cultures.

Alongside the recognition of spirits and spirituality outside of the con-fines of Western belief systems, ancestor recognition is another important precursor to Yemonja awakening in the United States. Wilson provides an important awakening moment connecting the recognition of the world of the spiritual with connection to the ancestral presence of her father. The account of this experience appears in the *The Banner of Light* on November 12, 1870:

> Mrs. Hattie Robinson, formerly Hattie Wilson, gave a narrative of her develop-ment as a medium, but which she had been brought into acquaintance with her father in the spirit-life, who was her almost constant companion. He had told her, in detail, the circumstances of her early life, and upon inquiry of the persons names by him, still living in form, found them correct in every particular.
>
> Doubting to her is impossible, and has been for many years, and when your spiritual senses are opened, you will know that the spirit-world is not afar off, in space, but here in our midst. (*Banner of Light* 1870, 28.8, 2)

Diane Stewart rightly observes the fact that "there is continuity between the visible and invisible domains of human and ancestral world[s] . . ." (Stewart 2005, 140). Moving rapidly through the works of African American female writers, the recognition of the ancestor and the ancestral connection to spiritual recognition appear in a remarkable number of texts. Octavia Butler undertakes this theme in *Kindred* (1979) in which her character time travels between 1976 during the anti-Apartheid unrest in Soweto, South Africa, and slave-era Maryland in 1815. In keeping with the connection to Yemonja, during the first time-jump of Butler's protagonist, Dana, she finds herself on the banks of a river where she saves her white forefather for the first of many times. These rescues ensure he lives to rape her fore-mother, but they also ensure that Dana, herself, exists. Paule Marshall offers one of the most fully realized and beautifully articulated connection with ancestors in *Praisesong for the Widow* (1983). Marshall's principal character, Avey, experiences a physical memory of her ancestors during the *Maafa*. She feels "other bodies lying crowded in the her in the hot, airless dark," though she is alone in the space as she hears "their moans, rising and falling" during a short trip from Grenada to Carriacou (Marshall 1983, 209). Most importantly, however, the acknowledgment of their presence enables her to reclaim and redirect her own life. This ancestral awakening is also acknowledged in Phyllis Alecia Perry's *Stigmata* (1998), in which her protagonist connects spiritually and physically to her ancestors as the scars of their traumas mark her body in the twentieth century.

Perry's use of ritual processes to establish a cultural connection to the African-based traditional practices is also replicated throughout the creative production of African Americana. Richards emphasizes the importance of ritual process in "Let the Circle Be Unbroken: The Implications of African-American Spirituality":

> The spiritual is the foundation of all being because the universe is sacred. The universe was created, is continually "recreated," by a divine act. We participate in that act as we perform rituals in imitation of the Creator and aspects of the Creator (Olodumare and the Orisha, Onyame and the Abosom, and so forth). Through association with this sacred universe, divinely created, life itself becomes sacred and a most precious gift to be cherished, preserved, passed on and revitalized . . . . When we perform rituals as our ancestors did, we become our ancestors and so transcend the boundaries or ordinary space and time and the limitations of separation which they impose. When we call the spirits and they enter our bodies, we symbolize in our being the joining of, and therefore communication between, two spheres of the universe—"heaven" and the "earth." (252–254)

Still, accessing ritual processes in the African Diaspora has been complicated. In the initial conversations about this connection during the period of Reconstruction, Charles Chesnutt's conjure tales, which are always focused on the work of traditional practices of female spiritual workers, bridge nineteenth- and twentieth-century references to these practices.

The resonance of these ritual processes is present in American Voodoo praxis from the creation of mojo hands and other spiritual amulets to divination to everything between these popularized practices. In *Mama Day* (1988) and *Linden Hills* (1985) Gloria Naylor depicts ritual processes that are separated from their African epistemological meanings; however, these moments demonstrate an awareness of the African spiritual legacies of these processes. I see the most fully realized depiction of this kind of praxis in Toni Cade Bambara's *The Salt Eaters* (1980), in which the ancestors participate in a spiritual healing. It is noteworthy that Bambara's healer is called to the hospital to treat a patient that the medical doctor realizes that he cannot heal. As Hurston reminds us in *Tell My Horse: Voodoo and Life in Haiti and Jamaica* (1938), the spiritual landscapes of these island cultures are grounded in the recognition of African-descent spiritual rituals.

Hurston's work celebrated the multiple journeys, appearances, and syncretic manifestations of the energy of the African Divine that shape Santeria, Candomblé, Lucumí, and Voodoo cultures. These belief systems are intimately tied to the adherents of Ifá whom the Orisha protected on their journeys to the new world. They are contextualized by the recognition of the spiritual realm, the calling of ancestors, and the importance of ritual process that, as I note earlier, are recognizable components of African-based epistemologies. These awakenings elucidate the importance of the Yemonja awakenings that

I explore in this project as performed by Randy Weston and his collaborators, written by Octavia Butler and Tomi Adeyemi, and Spike Lee.

Randy Weston's ground-breaking opus, *Uhuru Afrika* (1961), was the result of a personal reclamation of his own African identity. His collaborators and co-spiritual travelers were Langston Hughes and jazz trombonist and composer, Melba Liston; both of whom were central to the creative process. Weston's collaboration with Hughes, Liston, and their multinational band represents a particularly resonant moment of Yemonja awakening because it generated a movement toward African Diasporan musical collaborations that transformed jazz and birthed Afrobeat. There is a strong correlation between the musical dexterity, flexibility, and fluidity of jazz and the multiple conceptions of the divine in African traditional belief systems. Weston, whose father taught him that he was "an African born in America," notes,

> All music began in Africa. All music began in Africa. The ancient Egyptians had schools of music. They were the first ones to write music. They were master instrument makers of harps and flutes and horns. So the whole concept of music was created in Africa and then spread to Europe and spread to other parts of the world. Most people don't understand or realize that . . . Wherever I go, I try to explain that if you love music, you have to know where it came from. Music was based upon spiritual values. In other words, you can't have a civilization unless they had music. African traditional societies have music for every single activity. So our ancestors brought that concept, even in slavery, they brought that concept to the Americas. So whether we were taken to Brazil or Cuba or Jamaica, whatever, that whole concept of Africa continues. All the names, whether you say jazz or blues or bossa nova or samba, salsa, all these names are all Africa's contributions to the Western hemisphere. (Weston 2013)

Among Yemonja's sacred objects are seashells, especially the conch shell, which connects her to music as well as the call-and-response, conversational component of jazz. In addition, it is difficult to separate jazz from its spiritual—and therefore, spatial—moorings. It is worth noting that jazz is based on the seminal number of seven—Yemonja's sacred number given its emphasis on three quarter time.

The three quarter time associated with jazz also connects with Randy Weston's composing practices. Weston began to use African drumming rhythms as the basis for his piano composition early in his career. Weston was a jazz icon and innovator from the 1940s until his death at the age of 92 on September 1, 2018. Less well recognized despite the quality and volume of her work, Melba Liston's career spanned three continents and the Caribbean. Born in Kansas City in 1926, she began playing the trombone at seven years. By the time she was eight years old, she was playing professionally. She was raised largely in Los Angeles, where Dizzy Gillespie went in search of her as he formed one of his bands in preparation for a 1956 State Department tour of South America.[1] Liston's legacy is inseparable from the space she inhabited in a male dominated industry, playing an instrument gendered as male, working as one of few women in this space. In celebration of the many layers of Yemonja, Liston cannot also be considered outside of the complications of sexuality, feminine power, and patriarchy. The collaborations between Weston and Liston bookended her career. In sum, they collaborated on ten albums together.[2] One of the most important collaborations resulted in one of the pivotal moments in the reclamation of the African feminine divine in Weston's *Uhuru Afrika* that was released in 1960. It was later banned in South Africa in 1964.

Uhuru Afrika is divided into an introduction and four movements representing the union and communion of Africa and the African Diaspora. Defined by what we now know as Afro-beat, *Uhuru Afrika* was among the most lauded amalgamations of African and African Diaspora music that we now associate with Weston, Fela Kuti, and the London-based Ghanaian group, Osibisa, among others. *Uhuru Afrika* was interdisciplinary in focus, involving a 24-piece big band that included jazz luminaries from across the African Diaspora. Liston arranged the music for the album. Hughes played pivotal roles as the author of the liner notes for the album, author of the introduction, entitled "Uhuru Kwanza," and co-author with Weston on the second movement, entitled "African Lady." The language of this lyric poem relates directly to the energy, spirit and essence of Yemonja. In the second stanza of the poem, Hughes identifies the "African lady" as the "Goddess of sun/And of sea." Even in the liner notes for the album, Hughes continues to reference the ocean, clearly acknowledging Yemonja. Hughes writes, "When Randy plays, a combination of strength and gentleness, virility and velvet emerges from the keys in an ebb and flow of sound seemingly as natural as the waves of the sea (Weston and Jenkins 2010, 90).

Key to these Hughes lyrics are his verdant references to Yemonja, as the orisha of the sea as the mother of the entire "world" of the Orisha. *Uhuru Afrika*, though, links us with the spiritual, African-centered female deity. In particular, the fourth movement incorporates many of the drum rhythms associated with dances associated with Yemonja in Santeria, Vodun, candomblé, and Lucumi cultural practices. Taken in its totality, *Uhuru Afrika* is an interdisciplinary and multisensory text that resonates with the sexual, spiritual, and divine empowerment associated with Yemonja. Her presence is infused in the artistic expression of Uhuru Afrika in its recognition of and connection to spirit, in the calling forth of the goddess in Hughes' lyrical poem, and in the ritual process sustained through the call of the drumbeats that Weston uses to reconnect with Africa as a space of belonging. Like Yemonja, the legacy of

the energy that *Uhuru Afrika* released cannot be contained. The energy created, then defined, the Afro-beat genre that spread throughout the Diaspora,
affirming the survival of the peoples touched by it, and their connection to
Africa.

I also see a Yemonja awakening in cultural dialogue that exists between
Octavia Butler's *Wild Seed* (1980) and Tomi Adeyemi *Children of Blood and
Bone* (2018). *Wild Seed*, though published last, is the beginning of Butler's
Patternmaster quintet, a series of novels that also includes *Patternmaster*
(1976), *Mind of My Mind* (1977), *Survivor* (1978), and *Clay's Ark* (1984). In
Wild Seed, Butler addresses the *Maafa*, European colonization and enslavement, and the Africans who participated in the trade in humans. Further, since
Wild Seed opens in Nigeria, the energy of the orisha shape the context of
the novel. Doro, Butler's antagonist, finds Anyanwu, the protagonist shortly
after he loses his "people" who were taken into the slave system after their
village was raided. An ancient, immortal, yet disconnected, spirit Doro can
only live by taking the body of another. He survives by stealing "the souls
of men" (Butler 1980, 13). In so doing, Butler predicates the condition of his
immortality as a spiritual corollary to the Transatlantic trade in humans and
Yemonja, as the orisha of the ocean, who traveled with them to the unknown.
Conversely, Anyanwu, an immortal shape-shifter, embodies the history of
the Africans who fled the expansion of the kingdom of Dahomey in Benin,
a nation whose growth was fueled by its participation in securing Africans
for the trade in humans. Butler captures this history writing, "We were . . .
subject to Benin before the crossing. Then we fought the Benin and crossed
the river to Onitsha to become free people, our own masters" (8–9). Doro also
embraces the notions of eugenics and colonization; he threatens Anyanwu's
family to coerce her into co-breeding a generation of differently abled offspring, controlled by his own desires of empire.

Yet, Butler disrupts the paradigm of empire-building writing by giving
Anyanwu the characteristics associated with Yemonja. Before the appearance
of Doro, Anyanwu has been living in her community as a healer, a recognized
goddess, as Butler notes, she is "a goddess, a woman through whom a god
spoke" (5). During her long relationship with Doro, however, she becomes
very much like his slave, trying to save her children from him while co-
creating generations of offspring with Doro who sought to build a line of
immortals. As both a goddess and an enslaved woman, akin to Yemonja,
Anyanwu travels with her offspring through their own version of the *Maafa*,
moving through time and space, from Africa to the Americas. Butler strengthens the connection to Yemonja when, at the end of the second section of the
novel, Anyanwu chooses to live freely away from Doro after he kills one
of their sons. Butler's Anyanwu, as shape-shifter, transforms into the form
of a dolphin, and maintains that form for a hundred years. As we know, the

dolphin is sacred to Yemaya the New World derivative of Yemonja; dolphins are among her protected symbols. While she is in this form, Doro is unable to locate her; she is safe within the protection of the ocean in the realm ruled by Yemaya and Olokun. Eventually, Anyanwu travels with her offspring from Africa to the Americas, finally settling in California where Anyanwu takes a "European name: Emma" because she "had heard that it meant grandmother or ancestress."[3] In *Wild Seed*, then, Butler focuses on embracing the African Feminine Divine in order to reclaim the connection to the African past. While she acknowledges the centrality of trauma of the *Maafa*, at this point in the Patternmaster quartet, the generational trauma that it created remains unresolved.

One of Butler's numerous literary progenies, Tomi Adeyemi, extends the conversation that Butler started here, however, in her award-winning debut novel, *Children of Blood and Bone*. The plot of the novel turns on a group of people, known as the maji, who are subjugated by the kosidan in Orisha, the mythical world and the structural lens that Adeyemi creates to respond, if you will, to Butler. The magical powers of the maji are connected to the Orisha; however, there power has literally been stolen by the kosidan king, Saran. In order to save her family and end the subjugation of the maji, Adeyemi's protagonist, Zélie, her brother, Tzain, and Amari, the daughter of King Saran, undertake a journey to return magic to the world. In effect, the three unlikely sojourners are tasked to clear the trauma that defines their lives by acknowledging the world of the spirit, reconnecting to their ancestors, rediscovering their lost ritual processes.

From the beginning of the novel, Adeyemi reverences and references the orisha acknowledged in Ifá. In addition to naming her mythical world Orisha, she names the clans of the maji appropriately. In the frontmatter of the novel, to cite on instance, we learn of all of the clans, including "Omi Clan Maji of Water, Maji Title: Tider Deity: Yemoja" (Adeyemi 2018, vi). Throughout the novel, Adeyemi calls the reader's attention to the importance of ancestry, not only for the maji characters, but also in her revelation that kosidan have maji ancestry. As importantly, she provides the origin story for Yemonja and disrupts the narrative of Western stories of creation. She writes:

Sky Mother loved all her children, each created in her image. To connect us all, she shared her gifts with the gods, and the first maji were born. Each deity took a part of her soul, a magic they were meant to gift to the humans below. Yemọja took the tears from Sky Mother's eyes and became the Goddess of the Sea . . . .Yemọja brought water to her human siblings, teaching those who worshipped her how to control its life. Her pupils studied their sister deity with unrelenting discipline, gaining mastery over the sea. (159)

Adeyemi uses Yemoja as one of the many spellings of the orisha's name, which appears variously as Yemanja, Yemojá, Yemana, in addition to other variations. In this contemporary re-creation of a mythical *camino* of Yemonja, Adeyemi creates a narrative through which her readers can simultaneously embrace an Afro-Futurist world and connect with the African Feminine Divine.

It is important to note that Adeyemi also focuses on the African origins of the orisha. Although Adeyemi is Nigerian-American, she asserts that she "never even imagined there could be black gods and goddesses. Seeing that image exploded my imagination wide open, and the world of Orïsha came to me pretty quickly . . . " (https://americanlibrariesmagazine.org/2019/06 /03/newsmaker-tomi-adeyemi/). Adeyemi "discovered" the Orisha when she encountered images of them in a gift shop in Brazil. Those who are drawn to the energy of the orisha recognize the immediacy of the connection that Adeyemi expresses here. In addition to Yemonja, Ògún, Sàngó, and Ochumare all appear in *Children of Blood and Bone*. The descriptions that Adeyemi uses in the text resonate with the traditional ways that orisha are depicted, as this passage demonstrates: "Yemọja's statue begins to glow, blinding in its shine. The light starts at her bare feet, travels up the curves and folds of her carved robes. When it reaches her eyes, her golden sockets glow bright blue, bathing the dome in its soft color. Ògún's statue shimmers to life next, eyes glowing in dark greens; Sàngó's comes in fiery reds; Ochumare's in bright yellows" (515). Yemonja, however, is one of the energies who appears in pivotal moments in the novel. Further, as Zélie, Tzain, and Amari traverse the mythical land of Orisha, Adeyemi also highlights the importance of the ritual processes that make this connection possible by including incantations in Yoruba in the novel. Adeyemi is clearly aware of the importance of the ancestors in the ritual process. She captures the position of the ancestor in Ifa, writing that the "power of . . . ancestors flows . . . grips onto our connection, onto the very heart of our blood" (517). Unlike Butler's *Wild Seed*, the ancestral connection in *Children of Blood and Bone* provides the context to heal the trauma of the *Maafa*.

For me, this is the central power of the novel, and the healing of trauma is the cultural work that this novel accomplishes. The spiritual intention of the novel is to heal not only the generational trauma associated with the aftermath of the *Maafa* but the contemporary trauma, as well. Adeyemi states that the "not-so-fun" inspiration for the novel was "when Trayvon Martin was shot, and . . . when *The Hunger Games* movie came out, and there was this bizarre backlash against the black characters because they were black" (https://americanlibrariesmagazine.org/2019/06/03/newsmaker-tomi-adeyem i/). *Children of Blood and Bone* unfolds through the journey of three young, untested people whose belief in the transformative power of ancestors, ritual process, and the Orisha is posited to save their world. The novel is energized as a means through which to heal cultural, generational, and contemporaneous trauma. It provides a pathway that makes the impossible possible.

To conclude, I turn to Spike Lee's Netflix series, *She's Gotta Have It* (2017 and 2019) as an ongoing Yemonja awakening because of the power of media to transform a particularly cultural moment. Although I would welcome having a debate about it, there is no escaping the fact that that *She's Gotta Have It* centers on masculinist paradigms, despite the fact that his central character, Nola Darling is a woman. A reprise of his ground-breaking 1986 film, this Netflix project focuses almost wholly on Nola, her artistry, her sexuality, and those with whom she is artistically and sexually entwined. As a self-described "sex-positive, polyamorous pan-sexual who doesn't believe in monogamy," Nola's sexual endeavors enable her to critique her artistry and, thereby, her life's purpose. However, Nola's responses to her sexual encounters with the three men who comprise her "three-headed monster" (Mars Blackmon, Jamie Overstreet, and Grier Childs) and her female lover, Opal Gilstrap, cannot escape the binary, single-sexed, heterosexist cultural imprint that defines our culture. Uninformed viewers, however, may miss the fact that Yemonja is a sexually powerful entity who, as mother of mothers, loves as she pleases.

Key to the portraiture of Nola, however, is Lee's inclusion of Ifá healing rituals in both seasons one and two of the series. Lee manages to play with all of the prevailing images of Yemoja as mother, as mermaid, sexually free, as Black and as mulatta, the latter symbolized by the presence of the Puerto Rican practitioner who administers the Yemoja healing. In season one, episode seven, "#LovDontPayDaRent," Lee introduces us to Lulu, Mars' sister, who is an Ifá practitioner. She oversees a cleansing ritual for Nola, in which she calls on both "Oshun" and "Yemaya." The inclusion of both of these powerful orisha are important because of the relationship between them. Yemonja is the mother of rivers and the mother of mothers. She is said to have birthed most of the orisha. In addition, she oversees all waters. Most importantly in reference to Lee's portraiture of Nola, Yemonja is the source of healing and protection. Although Yemonja is mother to Oshun, in other stories, they also share the relationship of sisters. Yemonja allows Oshun to oversee rivers. Oshun also invites her children to pursue dance and sensuality. Following this ceremony, Lee's Nola refines the ways in which she operates as lover, artist, and individual. She begins the process of centering herself outside of being commodified by gender and race. We are unsure, however, of whose child—Yemonja's or Oshun's—Nola really is.

Lee extends this conversation in season two, episode seven, entitled "#OhJudoKnow?" Set in Puerto Rico, this episode continues to explore Nola's reinvention. Mars' mother, Doña Tina, portrayed by Rosie Perez, reminds us that Puerto Rico is a "cathedral full of ancestors." This statement sets the tone for the ritual processes that Lee explores in this episode which relate in many ways to the narrative that Julie Dash undertakes in *Daughters of the Dust* as she reminds us that "the ancestor and the womb are one" (Dash *Daughters of the Dust* 2002). As is true of all moments of Yemonja awakening that I explore in this project, the narrative also remembers the trauma experienced by the African Diasporans who contributed to the cultural richness of the island's African-descent culture. Mars and Nola participate in a tour where they learn of the free Africans who came to the island before the Conquistadors killed off all of the Tainos, after which they came in chains. The tour guide reminds them "You will never hear that story told in history." On their journey, Nola notices a beautiful woman, dressed in gold, Oshun's color, who calls her "Oshun's daughter." Near the end of the episode, Nola and Mars encounter a fisherman wearing a face mask made of the blue beads associated with Yemonja who also refers to her as "Oshun's daughter." In this scene progression, Lee masterfully plays with the two different, but related pathways offered by Yemonja and Oshun.

Eventually, however, Lee has Nola and Mars join the other friends who traveled with them from New York on a beach at "Río Grande De Líoza," where the river meets the ocean—where the ocean—Yemaya—and a river—Oshun—meet. There, they dance to music played by traditional drummers. Eventually, the music changes to a traditional chant during which Nola has a spiritual transition. She dances with a child wearing the gold of Oshun as she moves ritually backwards into the water, then turns with her arms raised as the tide comes to her. She bows before the young girl who initiated her into the dance of Oshun; however, while the girl is dressed in gold, signifying Oshun, she wears a blue scarf, signifying Yemonja. The pathway, the *camino*, that Lee foreshadows requires that Nola complete a sacred journey to find herself. As M. Jacqui Alexander notes in *Pedagogies of Crossing* (2005), "Sentience soaks all things. Caresses all things, Enlivens all things. Water overflows with memory. Emotional memory. Bodily memory. Sacred memory" (Alexander 2005, 291). In this space, surrounded by two powerful energies of the African Feminine Divine, Nola is freed from the traumas that had defined her as a woman, an artist, and a sexual being.

Although Lee has not completed his portrait of Nola, I am persuaded that Lee's focus on Yemonja and Oshun may culminate in a transformation of Nola's character in keeping with the awakenings that the African Feminine Divine co-creates. The recognition of the African Feminine Divine supports the release of multiple layers of trauma and creates powerful spaces and new pathways to the possible. These pathways require that we acknowledge the realm of spirits, our ancestors, and the ritual processes that make these connections transformational. In my own spiritual practice, I begin and end each day by intentionally recognizing these connections. That this is possible, despite the numerous attempts to erase and denigrate African spiritual practices, is nothing short of phenomenal. Hurston, perhaps, characterizes it best when she writes, "A thing is mighty big when time and distance cannot shrink it" (Hurston 1938, 245).

NOTES

1. When member of the band complained that he had come all the way to California "for a bitch," Gillespie ordered the band play several bars of the complicated arrangement without "f-ing up," and when they failed, he defended Liston by saying, "Who's the bitch now?"
2. Liston suffered a paralyzing stroke in 1985. At the urging of Weston, she learned to compose and arrange music using a computer.
3. Yemonja is also known as the "mother of all mothers."

REFERENCES

Adeyemi, Tomi. 2018. *Children of Blood and Bone.* New York: Henry Holt and Company.
———. 2019. Interview. https://americanlibrariesmagazine.org/2019/06/03/newsmaker-tomi-adeyemi/.
Alexander, M. Jacqui. 2006. *Pedagogies of Crossing: Meditations on Feminism, Sexual Politics, Memory, and the Sacred.* Durham: Duke University Press.
Bambara, Toni Cade. 1980. *The Salt Eaters.* New York: Penguin Random House.
Banner of Light on November 12, 1870. Microfiche. Accessed May 27, 2003.
Butler, Octavia. 1977. *Mind of My Mind.* New York: Doubleday.
———. 1978. *Survivor.* New York: Doubleday.
———. 1979. *Kindred.* New York: Doubleday.
———. 1980. *Wild Seed.* New York: Doubleday.
———. 1984. *Clay's Ark.* New York: St. Martin's Press.
Dash, Julie. 1991. *Daughters of the Dust.* DVD. Directed by Julie Dash. United States: Kino International.
Hurston, Zora Neale.1938. *Tell My Horse: Voodoo and Life in Haiti and Jamaica.* New York: Harper Collins Publishers.
———. 1942. *Dust Tracks on the Road.* Philadelphia: J. B. Lippincott.
Jacobs, Harriet. 1861. *Incidents in the Life of a Slave Girl: Written by Herself.* Ed. L. Maria Child. https://quod.lib.umich.edu/cgi/t/text/text-idx?c=moa;idno=ABT6782.
Lee, Spike. 2017. *She's Gotta Have It.* "#LovDontPayDaRent." Netflix, 30 mins. November 23, 2017.
———. 2019. *She's Gotta Have It.* "#OhJudoKnow?" Netflix, 30 mins. May 24, 2019.
Marshall, Paule. 1983. *Praisesong for the Widow.* New York: Plume.

Naylor, Gloria. 1985. *Linden Hills*. New York: Penguin Books.

———. 1988. *Mama Day*. New York: Vintage Books.

Perry, Phyllis Alecia. 1998. *Stigmata*. New York: Hachette Books.

Richards, Dona. 1981. "Let the Circle Be Unbroken: The Implications of African-American Spirituality." *Présence Africaine* 117/118. Pré-Colloque du 3e Festival Mondial des Arts Nègres: «Dimensions mondiales de la Communauté des Peuples Noirs»/1st Pre-Colloquium of the 3rd World Festival of Negro Arts: «The World Dimensions of the Community of Black Peoples. 247–292.

Stewart, Diane. 2005. *Three Eyes for the Journey: African Dimensions of the Jamaican Religious Experience*. Oxford: Oxford University Press.

Weston, Randy, and Willard Jenkins. 1960. *Uhuru Afrika*. Roulette Records, album.

———. 2010. *African Rhythms: The Autobiography of Randy Weston*. Durham: Duke University Press.

———. 2013. Interview. https://www.allaboutjazz.com/a-fireside-chat-with-randy-weston-randy-weston-by-aaj-staff.php.

Wilson, Harriet. 1859. *Our Nig: Sketches from the Life of a Free Black*. http://www.gutenberg.org/ebooks/584.

Chapter 7

The Water of the Womb

The Unseen Power of Yemonja in James Baldwin's If Beale Street Could Talk

Michael Lindsay

James Baldwin's *If Beale Street Could Talk* is set in 1970s Harlem, New York. The protagonists' day-to-day interactions, living situation, potential for social mobility, and every aspect of their reality as African Americans is shaped by centuries of racial antagonism. Though Tish and Fonny are young and in love and are looking forward to a long life together, Fonny's arrest for a rape that he did not commit is a part of the legacy that his forefathers and foremothers had to endure by virtue of them being born Black in a society that demonizes the color of their skin. Tish and Fonny's struggle for dignity and freedom against a system of white supremacy makes the entire plot of the novel. Their love, determination, and sheer tenacity in the face of cruelty is a testament to the power of their ancestors who exhibited the same type of unfathomable strength in order to survive centuries of cruelty.

In the fifteenth century Portuguese ships took a small number of Africans from the continent's west coast. The demand for labor in the colonized Caribbean islands and North America would soon after create an increasing demand for Africans as slaves. Eventually, an estimated 12.5 million people were stolen from the shores of Africa and shipped across the Atlantic Ocean to the western hemisphere for the explicit purpose of economic exploitation. African men, women, and children were taken from the shores of their homelands and forced into the bellies of slave ships. Millions would survive the passage, untold millions would die while at sea and have their bodies thrown overboard, and others would throw themselves overboard to a certain death to escape an uncertain, but promisingly horrific future. Though Africans entered the bottom of slave ships without material possessions, they had not been divested of their culture. They would bring their memories, language, and culture with them, and these intangible artifacts would have lasting impressions on Black people for generations to come. "Perhaps one of the most significant areas of African influence on Blacks in the New World is religion" (Gordon 1979, 233). Like with their ancestors, religion would play a large role in the lives of enslaved Africans even though they transitioned into societies that would forbid their ancestral faith. One such faith that enslaved Africans brought to the New World was Ifá. Ifá is a spiritual system of the Yoruba people that includes science, epistemology, astronomy, cosmology, ontology, physics, mathematics, philosophy, and medicine (Washington 2012, 264). However, with the trauma of slavery and every imaginable and unimaginable evil associated with it, along with the passage of time, generations would see religious systems like Ifá interrupted, the memory of Africa blunted in the minds of African Americans, and much of the ontology of their religious system replaced with Western beliefs.

Though each generation of American born African would possess a dimmer cultural memory of life in Africa, the initial argument here is that aspects of Africa (the language, the ethos, the religion) would remain deep in the subconscious of Black people in America. Even though people were taken out of Africa for the purpose of slavery, Africa is never taken fully out of the people. Consequently, the underlying question in terms of religion is that though many Africans in America, through trauma and the passage of time, had forgotten the gods of their ancestors, had their gods forgotten them? For the purpose of my analysis of *If Beale Street Could Talk*, the answer to the question is no. The pantheon of gods in West Africa, more specifically the Orisha of the Ifá religion, followed their worshippers to the Caribbean and the Americas. Enslaved survivors of the Middle Passage appealed to Olokun to accept and bless their loved ones who had lost their lives on the ocean and sank to the deep, and petitioned Yemonja to alleviate their pain and suffering while at the mercy of unbearably cruel slave masters in the New World.

Yemonja is one of the most important female deities and occupies a high-ranking position in the Yoruba pantheon. She is celebrated as a giver of life and mother of all Orisha. Her name is a contraction of Yeye (mother), omo (child/children), and eja (fish), which translates to Mother Whose Children are the Fish, signaling her role as ruler of the rivers and divine protective mother of all. Her role as encompassing mother, protector of women, overseer of fertility, and comforter to her children is what draws Yemonja to the protagonist in *If Beale Street Could Talk*. In the novel Baldwin deconstructs the Christian metanarrative as it relates to Black people while subtly offering the protagonist a spiritual alternative that focuses on Black humanity by imagining both the Black body and the Black soul as sacred and unified. Though the main characters in *If Beale Street Could Talk* are generations removed from Africa and inundated with the historical consequences and contemporary reality of white supremacy, under the surface of their predicament is their unconscious, atavistic connection to Yemonja, who looks over them in the greatest time of need. This study examines Yemonja as unrecognized, yet present in the lives of the protagonist in *If Beale Street Could Talk* through their relation to the rivers, Tish's pregnancy, and the facilitation of spiritual growth.

THE WATER OF THE RIVERS

In part, Yemonja's breadth encompasses the western hemisphere because her enslaved worshippers bought her with them across the ocean into their new lives as chattel. In this study the major premise is that Yemonja's divine power stayed with her children even when she had been blotted from their memories and replaced with other gods. Africans enslaved in America gradually became more Christianized from the late seventeenth to the eighteenth centuries. The extent and effect of Africans being converted to Christianity is debatable and has been long studied. Du Bois says that " the first Afro-American institution, the Negro church. . . was not at first by any means Christian," and that "after the lapse of many generations the Negro church became Christian" (DuBois 1901, 498). Du Bois' analysis articulates the slow, meandering process of conversion by manner of alienation from one's own culture. Countee Cullen expresses the confusion and anxiety of Black people forgetting the gods of their ancestors and adopting new ones. He writes, "Quaint, outlandish hea-then gods,/ Black men fashion out of rods,/ Clay, and brittle bits of stone,/ In a likeness like their own,/ My conversion came high-priced,/ I belong to Jesus Christ" (Cullen [1925] 1995, 246). Though pointing to the cost of conversion acknowledges the tragedy of Christianization on the lives of Black people, Cullen further expresses the void that exist between a White Jesus Christ and his newly converted Black followers. Cullen places the subject at the altar of God but forlornly "Wishing He I served were black,/ Thinking then it would not lack,/ Precedent of pain to guide it," ultimately desiring that his god had "borne a kindred woe" (Cullen [1925] 1995, 247). The irony of not having a savior that shares the appearance and, by extension, the cultural heritage of the believer is not lost on the speaker. This predicament places the believer cut off from his heritage in a spiritual crisis in which the chasm created by the insertion of a foreign god is filled with curiosity, imagination, and guilt.

The blunted memories and traumatized psyches of African Americans may have erased their West African deities from the collective cultural conscious; however, goddesses like Yemonja still retain a presence in the subconscious of Black people who implement aspects of her divine nature into facets of their expression in a strange land. Namely, the life reaffirming impact of water that is a consistent theme in the art and religious imagination of Black people is the most prominent connection to Yemonja. For African Americans, the spiritual significance of water predates the Christian context of baptism and reaches back to their African heritage. "To Africans generally, water transcends its scientific properties or chemical composition (H_2O) as testable in the chemistry laboratory. The sacred quality of water has diverse symbolic meanings and applications in Yoruba religious traditions" (Ogungbile 1997, 21).

Yemonja, who symbolizes the sacred and mysterious nature of the water, represents an external mother whose "children are the fish." She is the source of all living creatures on earth; therefore, the metaphysical principle of water is a primary element of creation. In this context, since all life began in the ocean (the water), then for Africans enslaved in America the water had the ability to perform rebirth. For instance, the negro spiritual "Wade in the Water" has a veneer of Christianity; however, this song refers to the slave having the opportunity to be born again as a free person. The song appears sacred, but its message and intent are wholly secular for the African slave, as its message is rooted in the spiritual concept of the maternal aspect of the water.

The spiritual "Swing Low, Sweet Chariot" is also coded in Christian religious imagery but also makes direct reference to the Underground Railroad. The song's historical context is secular in that the literal meaning speaks of a physically tangible result. But, the lyrics, "I looked over Jordan, and what did I see, Coming for to carry me home? A band of angels coming after me, Coming for to carry me home," are sacred in the African context of the Jordan River having the power to transform those willing to cross it (*The New National Baptist Hymnal* (Nashville: National Baptist Publishing, 1977, 486). Even Christian hymns that would resonate with Black people like "Near the Cross" associate the crucifixion of Christ with the redemptive properties of water: "Jesus, keep me near the cross—There a precious *fountain*; Free to all, a *healing stream*, flows from Calvary's mountain. In the cross, in the cross be my glory ever, Till my raptured soul shall find rest, *beyond the river* [my emphasis] (Crosby 1977, 94)."

From Africans landing in port cities on the eastern seaboard, to runaway slaves having the Mississippi, Tennessee, Chattahoochee, Savannah, and Potomac Rivers as obstacles to their freedom, the rivers have had deep physical and spiritual significance to Black people in America. Yemonja is originally the patron deity of the Ogun River in Nigeria, but her worship and domain were expanded to the ocean where she creates a symbiotic relationship with Olokun, the Yoruba ocean deity. This convergence of spiritual forces is present when Africans arrive to the shores of America. And, Yemonja's presence becomes cross-continental as her children are no longer worshipping her at the rivers, lakes, and streams in West Africa, but are waiting, praying, and watching at the edges of rivers in the southern United States, in need of divine protection and intervention to cross those rivers and get to the other side to freedom. When Langston Hughes writes, "I've known rivers ancient as the world and older than the flow of human blood in human veins. . . My soul has grown deep like the rivers," it not only speaks to the spiritual connection that Black people have with these bodies of water, it also speaks to the experiential connection that unites Black peoples' origin with the flowing of the rivers (Hughes [1920] 1995, 257).

The river is where the protecting presence of Yemonja and the characters in *Beale Street* converge. The initial irony of Yemonja's unacknowledged influence of Tish and Fonny is the fact that Tish's last name is Rivers. By naming his protagonist Rivers, perhaps Baldwin, even unconsciously, is linking Tish to Yemonja from even before her infancy. In this sense, the words of Hughes, "I've known rivers ancient as the world and older than the flow of human blood in human veins," suggest that Tish's worldview is subconsciously influenced by an ancient perceptiveness (Hughes [1920] 1995, 257). This link is essential to Tish's survival as she seemingly disengages from the Christian spiritual system as she connects it with the hypocrisy and vileness of the American landscape. Tish explains, "I must say that I don't think America is God's gift to anybody—if it is, God's days have got to be numbered. That God these people say they serve . . . has got a very nasty sense of humor" (Baldwin 1974, 34). It is clear that Tish feels antagonized by the concept of God in the American context. This notion is essential when considering that Tish, though seemingly irreligious in the Christian context, is nevertheless spiritual in the African context. The first hint of her spirituality as connected to something beyond her knowledge is evidenced in her last name, Rivers. Secondly, the novel takes place between Harlem and the East Village, New York; therefore, Tish and Fonny are in close proximity to the divine presence of Yemonja as they are nestled between the Hudson and East Rivers.

Tish's connection to the rivers is also corroborated by her and Fonny's attempt to escape "death that was awaiting to overtake the children of our age" (Baldwin 1974, 44). Yemonja makes all life possible. With the trap of teaching the Black children to be like slaves, which would lead to their eventual deaths, the discriminatory and racist society intends for the same fate to befall Tish and Fonny (Baldwin 1974, 44). However, despite all of the obstacles "Fonny had found something that he could do . . . and this saved him from the death . . . And perhaps I clung to Fonny, perhaps Fonny saved me [Tish] . . ." (Baldwin 1974, 44–45). Their reality is consumed by the possibility of death, so, feeling abandoned by the Christian concept of God and yet maintaining a connection to spiritual principles, Tish makes room in her nuanced spiritual system for the protecting power of Yemonja.

Tish is keenly aware of the possibility of death and the fact that the symbols are all around her. The jail that Fonny is being held in is referred to as the Tombs (Baldwin 1974, 32) and Tish compares crossing the prison yard to visit Fonny to crossing the Sahara Desert (Baldwin 1974, 7). Here, the Sahara is an appropriate symbol of death insomuch as a desert would be void of water. However, Tish Rivers brings life to the desert, allowing Fonny to survive when others are dying all around him. As she walks through the prison yard, she is carrying life with her. In a literal sense she is carrying life because she is pregnant. Secondly, and perhaps most importantly, she recognizes the power associated with her pregnancy. Not only is she carrying life inside her womb, she also understands that the knowledge of pregnancy can potentially give Fonny the glimpse of hope he needs to survive the Tombs. Tish, even with an inability to consciously acknowledge Yemonja, does on some level recognize the divine nature of motherhood and that she not only has the ability to create life inside the womb but also has the ability to sustain life in the tomb.

Tish's recognition of the life-producing force of her pregnancy can be juxtaposed to Elizabeth in Baldwin's *Go Tell It on the Mountain*. Tish and Fonny are parallels to Elizabeth and Richard in *Go Tell It on the Mountain*. Richard and Fonny are arrested and jailed in the Tombs for crimes they did not commit. Elizabeth and Tish are pregnant, unbeknownst to their jailed lovers. The difference, however, is between Elizabeth and Tish's ideas about the impact of the news of their pregnancies on their lovers who, like the unborn children, are confined. Elizabeth chooses not to tell Richard of her pregnancy. Baldwin writes,

> She had made her great mistake with Richard in not telling him that she was going to have a child . . . But the circumstances under which she discovered herself to be pregnant had been such to make her decide, for his sake, to hold her peace awhile. Frightened as she was, she dared not add to the panic that overtook him. (Baldwin 1952, 162)

And, even though Richard is eventually released from the Tombs, he commits suicide, leaving Elizabeth to wonder what would have come of her making a different choice. Richard survives the Tombs, which, in the case represents death, but he carries this death with him even after his release. In effect, he spiritually died while in the Tombs.

Tish chooses to tell Fonny about her pregnancy, and, as a result of hearing the news, Fonny is given all the hope he needs to survive even after his release. When Tish delivers the news, she describes his reaction with water imagery. Immediately after she tells Fonny, "we're going to have a baby," she comments, "His [Fonny's] face looked as though it were plunging into water . . . my hands got wet on the phone and then for a moment I couldn't see him at all and I shook my head and my face was wet" (Baldwin 1974, 5). Fonny receiving the news of Tish's pregnancy being synonymous with water signals the connection to Yemonja. The Tombs, being compared to the Sahara, is impossible to survive without a source of water. Water is the origin and sustaining force of all life, and in Ifá, Yemonja is the goddess of the rivers, lakes, and streams, which will make her a necessity for survival in Fonny's predicament. Tish, whose surname beckons fertility and birth, brings water with her through the desert, and Fonny plunges into it when he receives the news of their baby.

THE WATER OF THE WOMB

Being placed between the East River and Hudson River spatially places the main characters in *Beale Street* within the surrounding presence of Yemonja. The symbolic connection to the meaning of the rivers is documented in the music and literature of their African American ancestors. Yemonja's presence is also with Tish in a familial sense through her surname. Tish, simply by possessing the name Rivers, symbolically brings water through the desert and consequently life to the dying. Moreover, her pregnancy fosters a deeper connection to Yemonja who is the divine mother spirit, the guardian of women, the ruler of motherhood. As Yemonja's domain is the water, often considered the birthplace of all life on earth, "she is directly related to the water that exists in the womb [which] . . . creates a limited stable environment for an embryo up until the moment of birth" (Fatunmbi 1992, 12).

Tish's pregnancy is integral to the plot of the novel. Fonny's imprisonment is amplified as the injustice of it is juxtaposed to the hope and promise of new life. The pregnancy is significant to every aspect of the story and her ability to thrive in this situation is imperative to both Fonny and the unborn child. However, considering the profound nature of Tish's pregnancy, the significance of it ultimately minimizes Tish's role in the overall narrative when examining it in the Christian context, and it is through Ifá that her significance can fully be appreciated. Within the Christian context, a pregnant Tish is an incubator, a vessel that will bring forth the novel's true blessing, the baby. Though the promise of new life is heavily significant to the story, Tish's role as a potential mother is perhaps even more significant because the unborn child depends on her survival. In the biblical context Tish is marginalized, and the emphasis is placed on Fonny's position as a prisoner, and Tish's ability to birth the child, which represents redemption. Tish is minimized through a biblical perspective because the Christian narrative is male-centered. According to the Bible, Adam, the male, is created first,

and he essentially gives birth to Eve, the female. God makes a covenant
with Abram, changing his name to Abraham, that he should be "the father
of many nations," even though Sarah would carry the child (Genesis, 17:4).
Jesus' lineage is traced through the biblical narrative from Seth, the son of
Adam and Eve, to Heli, the father of Joseph who married the virgin Mary.
Even though, according to the Christian narrative, Joseph is not the biological father of Jesus, it is his genealogy that readers follow from Genesis to the
New Testament while Mary's is ignored. Mary, as necessary and miraculous
as her story is, is introduced to the narrative to carry and birth the messiah
while Joseph is effectively introduced, through his family, at the beginning
of the biblical narrative.

In this patriarchal paradigm, Tish's role is reduced, the emphasis is solely
placed on Fonny, and the underlying assumption then becomes that she is
pregnant with a boy. By writing this novel from the point of view of Tish,
having her voice and perspective be the guiding light by which the audience
witnesses this story, Baldwin consequently offers a counternarrative to the
male-dominated idea of what a savior is. Tish is both mother and storyteller,
and this dynamic aligns the novel with an Afro-centric perspective by which
matriarchal paradigms are normalized. Fatunmbi writes:

> Ifá teaches that the visible universe is generated by two dynamic forces. One
> is the force of "inàlo," which means "expansion," and the other is the force
> of "isokì," which means "contraction." The first initial manifestation of these
> forces is through "ìmo," which means "light," and through "aimoyé," which
> means "darkness." In Ifá myth, expansion and light are frequently identified
> with Male Spirits called "Orisha' ko." Contraction and darkness are frequently
> identified with Female Spirits called "Orishá bo." (Fatunmbi 1992, 12)

Taking into account these dynamic forces emphasizes Tish's connection
to the female spirit, Yemonja. Through contraction and darkness Tish ties
together her unborn child and Fonny. In jail, Fonny is reduced, or contracted,
in a small cell devoid of natural light. Fonny, for almost the entirety of the
novel, is shrouded in darkness both literally and figuratively. Fonny's imprisonment is paralleled with his unborn child who, for almost the entirety of the
novel, is confined to the womb, a dark place. Yemonja represents the female
aspect of these forces because "she is directly related to the water which
exists in the womb. The water in the womb is contractive because it creates
a limited stable environment for an embryo up until the moment of birth"
(Fatunmbi 1992, 12). In addition, the expansion and light are associated with
Olokun, the masculine aspect of these dynamic forces which is essential to
the development of each character as well. Throughout the novel, Fonny and
his unborn child are moving toward the same fate, expansion into the light.

The Tombs are a place of darkness, and the bulk of the energy spent in the novel by the main characters is to get him released, or into the light. The child is confined to the womb constantly growing and coming closer and closer to life outside of the womb, or, into the light. Both characters, Fonny and the unborn child, need Tish and, since Tish is both Fonny's and the child's pathway to expansion and light, her alignment with the protective spirit of Yemonja is evident. Through this dynamic it is also evident that Yemonja and Olokun exemplify the relationship between water and birth, even if the birth is spiritual as in Fonny's case. Unlike most biblical narratives, the full weight of the story and its impetus lies with Tish, a woman.

Tish is able to be a protector to the baby and liberator to Fonny precisely because she is pregnant. Tish is sensitive to the influence of Yemonja because, according to Ifá, everything that has existence has consciousness; therefore "Water as a form of consciousness is that which flows and nurtures, it is consciousness that incubates and feeds, and it is the essence of Maternal Caring as it relates to the protection of children" (Fatunmbi 1992, 3). Tish is intuitively connected to another form of consciousness that grounds her in a hostile environment. By being grounded and self-assured, she has the strength to work through her pregnancy, comfort and reassure Fonny, battle racism, and face the prospect of death on a daily basis.

Baldwin also breaks the traditional male-centered narrative by making Tish and Fonny's first sexual encounter with each other both a physical and spiritual experience. To Baldwin "the flesh and the spirit are one" (Baldwin 1998, 754). Baldwin's ideology is diametrically opposed to what Kelly Brown Douglas defines as Platonized Christianity. According to Douglas, Platonized Christianity demands a "dualistic approach to distinguishing divinity from humanity and the soul from the body" (Douglas 2005, 28). In addition, "A platonized sexual ethic does not allow for sexual activity as an expression of an intimate, that is, mutually loving, relationship. For all intents and purposes, platonized Christianity severs sexual intimacy from intimate relationality" (Douglas 2005, 37). Douglas comments that "platonized Christianity perhaps found its most comfortable home in the evangelical Protestant tradition" (Douglas 2005, 37). Baldwin interrupts this faith tradition by making Tish and Fonny's sexual encounter a sacred moment. Immediately after they make love, Tish comments, "his sperm and my blood were slowly creeping down my body, and his sperm was on him and on me; and, in the dim light and against our dark bodies, the effect was as of some strange *anointing* [my emphasis]" (Baldwin 1974, 101). Tish's perception of their sex act completely ignores the Westernized Christian concept of the roles of the body and the soul and gives the Black body equal importance with the eternal soul. By rejecting the Westernized version of what is and isn't sacred, they override the racist ideology that provides a "foundation for easily disregarding certain bodies, but also allows for the demonization of those persons who have been sexualized" (Douglas 2005, 37).

Tish and Fonny are not devalued by their humanity as expressed through sex. Tish explains at the beginning of the narrative that she does not feel ashamed. When she discusses the feelings associated with having a loved one in jail, she states, "I think that, personally, I would be ashamed. But I've had time to think about it and now I think that maybe not" (Baldwin 1974, 8). She also states that people who do feel ashamed are wrong to feel that way and that "the people responsible for these jails should be ashamed" (Baldwin 1974, 8). Tish is intuitive enough to recognize that the societal structure is designed against poor people of color, and that the guilt of failure should fall in the laps of people who set the traps. More importantly, she recognizes that the shame that poor people feel leads to the death "that was waiting to over-take the children of our age" (Baldwin 1974, 44). She explains that "those kids aren't dumb. But the people who run the schools want to make sure they don't get smart: they are really teaching the kids to be slaves" (Baldwin 1974, 44). Instead, Tish is proud of Fonny and she refers to the end of their first-time making love as an *anointing*, which signals the experience as divine. When Tish and her mother, Sharon, prepare to tell Tish's father, Joseph, and her sister, Ernestine, about the pregnancy, Sharon orders Joseph to pour a very old bottle of French brandy. Just before she orders them to drink the brandy she says, "This is a sacrament" (Baldwin 1974, 54). Sharon's actions do call to mind the Last Supper, and by doing this she marks the pregnancy as sacred in nature and she uses the moment and the wine to symbolize the spiritual reality of the pregnancy. The religious imagery used by Tish and Sharon has a veneer of Christianity but cannot be Christian in the traditional sense since their sex act falls outside of the confinement of marriage and their baby was conceived and will be born out of wedlock. However, within the spiritual system of Ifá their black bodies are not devalued, they are not hounded and demonized by racism, and they are protected by the divine mothering spirit of Yemonja.

The Water of the Spirit

One of the most important callings of a mother is to make sure her children grow healthy so that once they are fully grown, they can flourish as they develop an awareness of self. As a maternal spirit, Yemonja's function is to nurture the growth of her children physically and spiritually. In the physical sense, the child growing in Tish's womb is the embodiment of growth. It is through the nurturing waters of the womb that Yemonja's presence is vital to the development of the child. The child's development is vital to the survival of Tish's whole family. Joseph, her father, says to her, "You lose that baby, and Fonny won't want to live no more, and you'll be lost and then I'll be lost, everything is lost" (Baldwin 1974, 197). And, once she comes to understand that coming to see Fonny in her pregnant state is bringing him joy she says, "And I understand that the growth of the baby is connected with his deter- mination to be free. So, I don't care if I get to be as big as two houses. The baby wants out. Fonny wants out. And we are going to make in happen: in time" (Baldwin 1974, 199). Yemonja, by protecting the child in the womb, is simultaneously stretching her providence to the rest of the family who see the child as a beacon of hope.

In a spiritual sense the growth these characters experience is most evi- denced through Fonny's transcendent journey while incarcerated. Early in his confinement Fonny is overtaken by fear. During one of Tish's visits, Fonny yells, "What we going to do about that fucking lawyer? He don't give a shit about me, he don't give a shit about *nobody!* You know what's going on in here? You know what's happening to me, to *me*, to *me*, in *here*?" (Baldwin 1974, 135). By the end of the novel, when Tish visits to tell him that they almost have the money to make his bail, she says that, despite the bruises, "I saw this question in Fonny's enormous, slanted black eyes—eyes that burned, now, like the eyes of a prophet" (Baldwin 1974, 236). Tish's description of Fonny's appearance echoes Moses descending from Mount Sinai after receiving the Ten Commandments from God, therefore pointing to Fonny's spiritual evolution. However, what is more significant than the change in his appearance is the change in his tone. Fonny says to Tish, "Listen, I'll soon be out. I'm coming home because I'm glad I came, can you dig that?" He continues, "*Now*. I'm an artisan . . . Like a cat who makes—tables. I don't like the word artist. Maybe I never did. I sure the fuck don't know what it means. I'm a cat who works from his balls, with his hand. I know what it's about now. I think I really do. Even if I go under. But I don't think I will. Now" (Baldwin 1974, 193). As stated previously, Fonny's survival and growth are dependent upon the growth of the baby still in the womb. Because Yemonja is connected to birth, the aspect of her dichotomy that nurtures life at the same time nurtures creativity since birth is the essence of creation. Therefore, as the baby grows in the primordial waters of the womb, so does Fonny's growth into full self-knowledge and self-acceptance.

Baldwin ends *If Beale Street Could Talk* with Sharon telling Tish that Ernestine has Fonny's bail money. Before she can respond, Tish receives the news that Frank, Fonny's father, committed suicide and that his body was found "way, way, way up the river, in the woods" (Baldwin 1974, 197). At the moment Tish screams as the baby is about to come. Then, the novel ends with Tish envisioning Fonny sculpting wood and stone. Ironically, or perhaps not, the timing of Frank's death coincides with Fonny's release from jail and the baby's release from the womb. Here, the water imagery of Frank being

found up the river and Tish's water breaking ties Yemonja to the resolution of
the narrative. Yemonja does not require human sacrifice when petitioning for
her help; however, considerable deliberation could be given to the symbolism of Frank's death in relation to Fonny and his grandchild's expansion into
the outside world and out of the darkness. For certain, Tish's waters had to
break in order for the child to be born, and perhaps symbolically the breaking waters of the womb are enough to release Fonny from his cell as well.
However, Frank's death by the river does not necessarily speak to the sacrifice to a god, but more to the acknowledgment of the enormity of the situation
and a refusal to exist in a system that refuses to allow him to accept himself.

The recurrent theme in this study has been the presence and influence of
Yemonja in the lives of the protagonists in *If Beale Street Could Talk*, and by
extension a co-narrative that exists about the presence and influence of divinity in the lives of Black people even when the divine is not openly petitioned
or worshipped. In an existential sense, does a god's love need to be recipro-
cated? More specifically, in the case of Yemonja, how far and long does a
mother hold on to her missing children. In this study, the primary argument
is that she holds tight to Tish and Fonny though they are generations removed
from the knowledge of her existence. There is no evidence to suggest James
Baldwin's intent for any of his work was to point his Black audience toward
their ancestral gods and goddesses. Baldwin was, however, exceptionally
critical of the Western Christian faith tradition, and in his fictional works
like *Beale Street*, *Go Tell It on the Mountain*, and the *Amen Corner*, and in
his essays like *The Fire Next Time*, he strongly and eloquently suggests in
so many ways that the same type of religion that justifies and sustains white
supremacy cannot liberate Black people. And, with that refrain running
throughout *Beale Street*, with extraordinary subtlety he leaves room for the
Orisha who left the shores of West Africa to guide, comfort, and protect their
stolen children.

REFERENCES

Baldwin, James. 1974. *If Beale Street Could Talk*. New York: Signet.
———. 1998a. "Go Tell It on the Mountain." In *Early Novels and Stories*, edited by
Toni Morrison, 1–216. New York: Library of America.
———. 1998b. "The Fire Next Time." In *Collected Essays*, edited by Toni Morrison,
291–347. New York: Library of America.
———. 1998c. "White Racism or World Community." In *Collected Essays*, edited
by Toni Morrison, 749–756. New York: Library of America.
Crosby, Fannie J. 1977. "Near the Cross." In *The New National Baptist Hymnal*.
Nashville: National Baptist Publishing Board.

Cullen, Countee. 1995. "Heritage." In *The Portable Harlem Renaissance Reader*, edited by David Lewis, 244–247. New York: Penguin Books.

Douglas, Kelly Brown. 2005. *What's Faith Got to do With It?: Black Bodies/ Christian Souls*. New York: Orbis Books.

Du Bois, W. E. B. 1986. "The Souls of Black Folk." In *Du Bois: Writings*, edited by Nathan Huggins, 357–547. New York: Library of America.

Fatunmbi, Awo Fá'lokun. 1992. *Yemoja/Olokun: Ifá and the Spirit of the Ocean*. New York: Original Publications.

Gordan, Jacob U. 1979. "Yoruba Cosmology and Culture in Brazil: A Study of African Survivals in the New World." *Journal of Black Studies* 10, no. 2: 231–244. http://www.jstor.org/stable/2784330.

Hughes, Langston. 1995. "The Negro Speaks of Rivers." In *The Portable Harlem Renaissance Reader*, edited by David Lewis, 257. New York: Penguin Books.

Ogungbile, David Olugbenga. 1997. "Water Symbolism in African Culture and Afro-Christian Churches." *Journal of Religious Thought* 53/54, no. 2: 21–38. https://search.proquest.com/docview/222072267?accountid=10139.

"Swing Low, Sweet Chariot." 1977. *The New National Baptist Hymnal*. Nashville: National Baptist Publishing Board.

Washington, Teresa N. 2012. "Mules and Men and Messiahs: Continuity in Yoruba Divination Verses and African American Folktales." *Journal of American Folklore* 125, no. 497 (Summer): 263–285, 390. http://ezproxy.clayton.edu:2048/login?url=https://ezproxy.clayton.edu:2230/docview/1081827135?accountid=10139.

Chapter 8

Spirit, Passion, and Sufferance

Articulations of Yemaya through Janie Crawford in **Their Eyes Were Watching God** *and Velma Henry in* **The Salt Eaters**

Khalilah Ali

Velma Henry in Bambara's *The Salt Eaters* and Janie Mae Crawford in Hurston's *Their Eyes Were Watching God* are women who defy the status quo. Although both novels are set in Black towns in the southeastern United States, *The Salt Eaters*, in fictional 1970s Claybourne, Georgia, and *Their Eyes* in mid-twentieth-century Eatonville, Florida, the authors each craft distinct narratives around two transgressive Black female characters. Colonial narratives around the Black female body have rendered it, contradictorily it seems, as both over-sexualized and undersexualized. A decolonial project like this one then, must seek to dispel the dichotomous femininity celebrated in the dominant discourse: one uplifted in the hegemonic order—the virgin; while the others are demonized—the whore and witch. Hegemonic notions of womanhood implore women to perform a brand of femininity privileged in the white masculinist imagination—the domestically pure mother-wife. Unfortunately, this idea has extended itself into orisha worship. Pérez argues that Yemaya's association with blackness and/or Africaness in Afro-Cuban tradition is not just about acknowledging her origin in Yorubaland. Instead, the emphasis on Yemaya as *Negra* (in contrast to Oshun as *Mulatta*) is rooted in the Mammy archetype associated with the robust heavy-set Black nursemaid figure canonized in the imagination of adherents to the slavocracy discourse. The racialized limiting characterization of Yemaya also works to deny the other voracious aspects of the deity: "Dozens of publications call Yemayá 'the universal mother,' implying a uniformity of ideal maternal traits across cultures; they define her sexuality primarily in terms of her desire to engender life as the 'marine matrix' of the cosmos" (Pérez 2013,

9). Accordingly, Yemaya is venerated as the embodiment of motherhood, giving and abundance—and, on the surface, Hurston's and Bambara's protagonists can be viewed as metaphors for the matronly nurturing aspects the deity represents. However, by examining these two characters and Yemaya more deeply, we are able to challenge the ways in which Black women are often celebrated only for their nurturing capacity. Like Yemaya, the mother identity is only one way in which Velma and Janie manifest their true selves. Thusly, these characters allow readers to imagine a transgressive feminine identity that not only represents the mother archetype but also shows the ways in which desire and violence, although not often viewed as traits analogous with femaleness, are also embodied in constructs of the feminine divine. By accessing Yemaya's various avatars, roads or paths as metaphoric mediums, I emphasize her multitudinous manifestations to challenge the static feminine ideal and to demonstrate the ways in which Janie Crawford and Velma Henry access rooted spiritual traditions to reshape understandings of what constitutes femininity. The various articulations of Yemaya are employed to demonstrate how the novels' female protagonists challenge the controlling limiting images of Black womanhood to experience sisterhood, sensuality, and sometimes suffering in order to become full complex and dynamic human beings.

Until Hurston, the idea of a transgressive sexual Black American female body was just that—transgressive. Janie's early regurgitated and enforced femininity, by her grandmother and husbands later, starkly contrasts with her latter widowhood emboldened through her dalliances with Teacake. Weir-Soley offers a sort of neo-hoodoo as a paradigm that rearranges Black female sexuality embodied in Janie's signifying or parodying femininity later usurped by a forbidden blackened marginalized femininity; a liberated Africanized sexual self, replete with some Eurocentric shaping around the eroticism of darkest Africa, still creates a decolonial transgressive understanding of the Black female body, which in many ways is well centered within Africanists' shifting of sexualized narratives of Africanity. By accessing African traditional spirituality, Bambara furthers this challenge in her invocation of *Lwa* in *Salt Eaters* but in interesting ways—although hoodoo and Vodou are centered in these works—I reframe the reading of both works through a Lukumí perspective. The following draws on my work around womanist epistemologies as they came to be revealed in diasporic literature and decolonial and queer theories. Further, my involvement in the Lukumí religion came from my interests in syncretic religion, specifically as it relates to Islam and African traditional religion, but first through my studies in the Caribbean of Vodou and Obeah. As an aborisha, a practitioner of the Lukumí tradition of the Yoruba spiritual system, I received implements to increase my participation and practice in the Lukumí system, but the status limits my knowledge, as a priestess is imbued with more ritualized secrets of the tradition. Therefore, my knowledge is supplemented by academic study and shaped by Pataki, Lukumí proverbs or sacred stories that explain the relationship between the Odu, corpus of religious texts, and Yemaya specifically, shared by my elders-priest/priestesses of Yemaya under whose tutelage is from who the bulk of my knowledge comes. I do access academic texts, popular trade works, and oral tradition in my analysis. Yemaya is often associated with the more privileged and accepted aspect of femininity—the mother. Unfortunately, in the diasporic tradition of Yoruba religious practices such as Lukumí, this particular privileging of the mother identity is rooted in colonized ways of knowing. Throughout Yorubaland, and later shifting into the New World, Yemaya's multiple roads or *caminos* were well known. Using Pérez' work as a grounding point, my queering of Hurston's and Bambara's texts for analytic purposes is not simply a project in opposing narratological heteronormativity; instead, I purport that Yemaya, in and of herself is not, in the pre-colonial imagination, transgressive sexually. Unfortunately, colonial overlays have created a binary between Yemaya and Oshun as well as Yemaya and Yemaya(s) that had not existed in the Ifa tradition (Pérez 2013, 13–14). Thus, what we understand as gender roles and the performance of them, as related to Orisha, are mostly embedded in the metanarrative of patriarchal colonial desire. To return to and embrace the complexity of gendered and sexual presentations of Orisha is therefore a decolonial project.

In *Pataki of Orisa and Other Essays for Lucumi Santeria*, Omi contends that Yemaya possesses a multitude of incarnations known in the Lukumí tradition as *caminos*—roads or paths. Each incarnation has a marginally distinct orientation and emblematizes water of various forms and locations (Omi 2009; Washington 2005). Yemaya's major identity is that of mother, but the Orisha's other archetypes include warrior, diviner, witch, rape survivor, jealous mournful lover, divorcee, and betraying sister. The spellings vary across practitioners and scholars, but I have standardized the spellings (Lukumí spellings) for this essay and access both Omi's and Washington's presentations of the roads of Yemaya. In the Odu Eyeunle Odi, Yemaya Ibu Akinomi, means "when upset she could destroy the world.' Yemaya is depicted as half sea creature and half human and can be found in the cusp of the peak of oceanic waves. Omi states that her implements include a fan, a sword, a dagger, an ax, and her colors are dark blue and light blue and green. Found in betwixt the seaweed of the seafoam, Yemaya Ibu Konla is seen in Odu Oddi-Eyila as a shipwright and poet (Washington 2005, 44). Yemaya Ogunosomi, a warrior of the ilk of Shango and Ogun, is born, or first spoken of, in Odu Iroso-Obara and lives on top of the waters and uses two machetes. Yemaya Okuti is the queen of the Aje, and this *camino* is temperamental and violent; this aspect of Yemaya is also a warrior who battles alongside Ogun.

Next, Yemaya Ibu Agana, represents fury and insanity, and is often associated with Olokun (a deep ocean deity) who lives at the very bottom of the ocean—she is a dancer often accompanied by snakes. Another manifestation, Yemaya Mayelewo's name means "the one who loves money and business." A favorite of Olodumare, Yemaya Mayelowo colored the waters of the ocean.

Collins argues that the larger society often entirely perceive Black women via the controlling images of the Mammy, Jezebel, Sapphire, matriarch, bitch, or welfare queen. Adherents to such deficit views cling to these images to condone the marginalization of Black women. Lee argues that it is the duty for women writers in some ways to be Erotic Revolutionaries and "stir up gender trouble, generate gender maneuvering, and bring wreck, into the public square by providing a *variety* of images [emphasis mine] and narratives as themes accessible to confronting, redrafting, and recoding gender expectations on sexuality" (Lee 2010, 9). Older women are often left out of any discussion around passion, sex, and sexuality. Resultantly, less has been done to "bring wreck" and recode the Mammy or to even address the matriarch or mature woman as a sexual being. Although modern and contemporary African American women authors have done much to complicate the public personification of Black femaleness in popular discourse, the dispassionate, matronly, asexual imagery of mature Black women, exemplified by Yemaya, and the oversexed Jezebel represented by Oshun are still pervasive.

Gates in the afterward of the 1990 reprint of the quixotic novel entitled "Zora Neale Hurston: 'A Negro Way of Saying'" contends Zora Neale Hurston is the standard-bearer of Black women's writers: Hurston became a metaphor for the Black woman writer's search for tradition.

> The craft of Alice Walker, Gayle Jones, Gloria Naylor and Toni Cade Bambara bears, in markedly different ways, strong affinities with Hurston's. Their attention to Hurston signifies a novel sophistication in Black literature: they read Hurston not only for spiritual kinship inherent in such relations but because she used black vernacular speech and rituals, in ways subtle and various, to chart the coming to consciousness of black women, so glaringly absent in other black fiction. (Gates 1990, 186)

The cultural sisterhood through the centering of Black women's experience and the use of vernacular and ritual, evident in these two novels, allows for abundant fruit for comparison. Janie Mae Crawford in Hurston's foundational text *Their Eyes Were Watching God* and Velma Henry in Bambara's *The Salt Eaters* summon the spirit, sexuality, and passion through the development of their main characters. In the African diasporic traditional spiritual system of Lukumí, often referred to as Santeria, an *espiritista* is a healer who serves as a medium for spirits and is adept at soliciting the aid of munificent spirits and banishing any malicious ones that seek to harm the adherent. Using the motif of summoning and banishing spirits, I am employing Yemaya to replace the problematic binary archetypes.

Washington contends that one of the significant aspects of Yemaya is her emphasis on the importance of relationships between women, as exemplified by Iyami Aje. Critics of Hurston's *Their Eyes Were Watching God* center the relationship between Janie and her lovers, but they tend to deemphasize the relationships with other women, including Janie's relationships with her grandmother Nanny Crawford and her best friend Pheoby Watson. *Their Eyes* is constructed as a frame narrative that serves to set the stage for and emphasizes the second yet primary narrative and the work begins with a conversation between Pheoby and Janie: "Pheoby, we been kissin' friends for twenty years, so Ah depend on you for a good though. And Ah'm talking to you from dat standpoint" (Hurston 1990, 7). The nature of the kitchen table talks that occurs between Janie and Pheoby, who "visited back and forth and once in a while sat around the lakes and fished (Hurston 1990, 88), serves as the work's exposition and emphasizes the sharing of women. Readers even underplay the more problematic relationships in our readings, including Janie's relationship with Nanny Crawford, the mother who abandoned her, the Eatonville townswomen who gossip about her and even Mrs. Turner who is enamored by an equally light-skinned Janie. Women characters throughout the novel seem to manifest an aspect of Yemaya Ibu Agana, jealousy, as they often glare at Janie enviously, "The women took the faded shirt and muddy overalls [Janie wore] and laid them away for remembrance. It was a weapon against her strength and if it turned out of no significance, still it was a hope that she might fall to their level one day" (Hurston 1990, 2). The women of Eatonville's jealousy is palpable, and they enjoy watching what they view as Janie's fall from grace. Pheoby, Mrs. Sumpkins, Pearl Stone, and Lulu Moss gossip about Janie after her return from the Everglades. While Pheoby defends her friend Janie, contending the women were "mad 'cause she didn't stop and tell us all her business,'" the others continue to demonize her for her relationship with the much younger Tea Cake: "She ain't even worth talkin' after," Lulu Moss drawled through her nose. "She sits high, but she looks low. Dat's what Ah say 'bout dese ole women runnin' after young boys" (Hurston 1990, 3). Although these relationships may not seem to be the most nurturing, the relationships between female characters certainly shape the characterization of Janie and help readers understand the inner workings of women's lives and serve to decenter the male gaze.

Bambara's work also emphasizes the relationships between women, and in fact, Bambara uses sisterhood as necessary for healing as a central thematic plot device. Velma Henry, representing the Yemaya Ibu Akinomi aspect, wants to die. Her relationship is a wreck as is her activist and professional life. However, after a suicide attempt, the community's women at the city of Claybourne's infirmary, led by healer Minnie Ransom and her army of spirits, or haints, and *Lwa* come to Velma's aid. The novel presents personal wholeness, political wholeness, and personal and social well-being as "all of a piece" (Kelley 1983, 484). Minnie Ransom, the manifestation of Yemaya Okuti, the witch, asks Velma Henry if she wants "to be well" (Bambara 1980, 3), and adds "'just so's you're sure, sweetheart, and ready to be healed, cause wholeness is no trifling matter. A lot of weight when you're well' (10) we become aware that 'wholeness' relates to balance, to a sense of all the parts working together" (Kelley 1983, 484). Velma's godmother M'Dear is the boarding house owner in Claybourne and has stood by Velma during her hospitalization at the town's hospital Southwest Community Infirmary. M'Dear with her mother-wit embodies the matronly aspect of Yemaya but as a businesswoman, she represents the Mayelowo aspect as well. M'Dear serves as a member of the prayer group that supports Minnie's work with Velma. Characterized as a warm stern woman who is revered in the small community, M'Dear, whose name is an abbreviation of 'my dear' or 'mother dear,' is a manifestation of the Iyaami *iya*-mother and *-mi* great. Meadows, the town's new white doctor, realizes the significance of M'Dear whose name he misheard to be ironically *Nadir*—an allusion to historian Rayford Logan's *Nadir of American Race Relations*, the point in America from the end of Reconstruction to the early twentieth century when racism was particularly insidious—or, a reference to Velma's own personal (and perhaps the town's) nadir, lowest point, when he asks the men in the poorer side of town if they knew M'dear. Bambara suggests that the current condition of the community represents the worst era for Claybourne's inhabitants. When Meadows mispronounces M'Dear's name, the local Welfare Men, not acknowledging or seeming to understand the connotations of Meadow's naming error, quickly correct him. Furthermore, M'Dear's role appears to be that of a confidante and guide for Velma; someone in whom she confides, thus allowing for the revelation of Velma's dreams, thoughts, and intentions. While wondering around the Infirmary, Velma shares a dream which M'Dear adeptly interprets. Sophie points out her political connections in similar language, wondering, "What the hell, Vee, did you think you were doing cutting on yourself and trying to die in an oven? And with so few seasoned workers left. Whop!" (Bambara 1980, 152). The linguistic parallel reinforces the recursive connection between personal and the communal hardships.

The Seven Sisters represent the diverse Yemaya identities as spread throughout the diaspora. The Seven Sisters first appear in the novel on Fred Holt's bus, and the multicultural dance troupe travels to Claybourne to perform during the town's spring festival. Their dialogue is ambiguously unassigned to individual speakers, suggesting a hodgepodge of conversation and identity. During their bus ride, a troupe member wisely emphasizes interconnectedness: "because the material without the spiritual and psychic does not a dialectic make" (Bambara 1980, 64). As Fred eavesdrops, their individual identities blend as "they rambled, interrupting each other, finishing off each other's sentences" (Bambara 1980, 68). In this scene, and in a later scene in the cafe, the Seven Sisters are identified individually, yet they function as a unit. Without sacrificing the distinctiveness of their own ethnic identities, the women are fused. The Seven Sisters represent the Iyami Aje. At different points, these characters represent magic, domesticity and the power of the feminine divine. It also presents non-hierarchical, non-dominating relationships that demonstrate matriarchal alternatives possibility. Called by names that allude to their different ethnicities, Nilda, Chezia, Mai, Inez, for example, or by subsistence food-linked cultural designations, the sisters of the yam (which is adimu or sacrificial offerings for most roads of Yemaya), plantain, rice, corn, etc., these women work and play together. They devise murals, songs and plays, which reflect the patron of poetics Yemaya Ibu Konla. While a Sister may leave to pursue another aspect of her life, as Inez does, the family "continues because she selects, or the troupe finds, a replacement" (Kelley 1993, 487). The performance troupe travels to Claybourne not only to stand beside Velma as she recovers but also to symbolically usher in the matriarchal order, which will allow Claybourne to reclaim the intended metaphysical healing powers entrenched in its soil. The unifications of these roads of Yemaya are an important metaphor for women's journey from a fragmented disjointed mass to a dynamic but empowered collective.

The role of *Lwa*, mud mothers, and "haints" in the search for well-being are pivotal to the plot's progression. Bambara emphasizes the importance of the spirits of the deceased, especially the founders of the town, throughout the work. In African and African American traditional folk-practice, the dead or *egun*, ancestors, have immense importance in Yoruba practice. According to scholars, the folk tradition of hoodoo, a new world manifestation of West African spirituality, is also steeped in veneration and work with the dead. Hoodoo practitioner Minnie Ransom and representation of the Iyami Aje often chats with old mother, her spirit guide. Bambara refers to the African deities in the novel as Loa (*Lwa*) who appear to have a role in the unfolding and outcome of the novel's events. "*Lwa*" is a term used to describe some of the West African deities brought to the new world by enslaved Africans and venerated in the traditions of Vodou in Haiti, Obeah throughout the West Indies, Santeria in Cuba and Candomblé in Brazil. Bambara refers to the gods as *Lwa* but her spellings, Oshun, Yemaya and Shango, more readily represent those of Lukumí. When readers are introduced to Minnie and her spirit guide Old Wife, we are also introduced to the *Lwa* who appear to be going on with their unspecified work as the novel's activity unfolds. The *Lwa* exist in the groves and countryside, and Bambara often invokes the spirits to direct the reader to the spiritual otherworld that exists alongside the physical world of Claybourne, Georgia.

It seems most likely to present Janie as a metaphor for the Erzulie the *Lwa* of love or the Yoruba deity of sensuality Oshun when making a comparative analysis. Janie, like Oshun, appears to possess features associated with the "mulatta" a pejorative for biracial women—narrow features and long hair:

> Ochun [*sic*] has long been portrayed as a "refined," "high yellow" woman able to "pass" as white and enter otherwise forbidden social spaces, due to her color, physiognomy, and deportment." Accordingly, Ochun craves caramel, syrup, and honey, a prized commodity, suggesting a life of leisure, while Yemaya receives food offerings strongly reminiscent of plantation rations and the slave diet, most notably unfiltered cane syrup and molasses. In popular cultural texts that owe less to odu than to nineteenth-century literary costumbrismo, Ochun stoops to the role of frivolous coquette, and Yemaya, that of noble drudge. (Perez 2013, 12)

The novel opens up with Janie fantasizing about love with a young boy and her coquettish flirtations set off the action of the work, "Through the pollinated air she saw a glorious being coming up the road. In her former blindness, she had known him as shiftless Johnny Taylor tall and lean. That was before the golden dust of pollen had beglamoured his rags and her eyes" (Hurston 1990, 11). Hurston later shifts this caricature, despite her biraciality by her invocation of spring and fertility, aspects associated with Negra (black) Yemaya, as an extended metaphor throughout the novel to represent Janie's reemerging yet socially transgressive sexual awakenings and rejection of a gendered and racialized caste system. The male characters are quick to take notice of a young Janie's feminine charms: "The men noticed her firm buttocks like she had grape fruits in her hip pockets; the rope of black hair swinging to her waist and unraveling in the wind like a plume; then her pugnacious breasts trying to bore holes in her shirt. They, the men, were saving with the mind what they lost with eye" (Hurston 1990, 2). In this moment, we are introduced through the first of such awakenings as Janie admires the local boy who Nanny witnessed "lacerating her Janie with a kiss" (Hurston 1990, 11)—the kiss serves as a catalyst for Nanny's desire to marry Janie off in a misunderstood effort, by Janie at least, to protect her. Although still recognized for her proximity to whiteness, the tryst taints Janie and castes her from *mulatta* Oshunesque "frivolous coquette" (although this characterization of Oshun itself is oversimplified) to Negra Yemayaness or the pejorative "noble drudge" conjured in the colonial imagination. Nanny is aware of the male lust, directed toward her granddaughter and laments, "I don't want no trashy nigger, no breath-and-britches, lak Johnny Taylor usin' yo body to wipe his foots on" (Hurston 1990, 12). Making Janie a "proper-women," as dictated by the times, became Nanny's duty and impoverished Black men would not do. Nanny Crawford, believing she is working in Janie's best interests, marrying-off of the young woman off to the much older Logan Killicks, not only allows Hurston to depict the substantial ways in which women relate to each other but also allows the author to convey the ways in which Janie's sexuality moves from immature seductress to mature exploitable mammy. Janie embodies the interdependency of Oshun and Yemaya, both Aje and both water Orisha, and the ways in which their roads often intersect in Pataki. The ease of transition also represents the mutability of blackness in the Western colonial imagination codified through the one drop rule that regards all African descended women as Black and therefore subject to domination and drudgery—Hurston's "mule of the world."

Conversely, the transition for Velma in *The Salt Eaters* is not the radioactive destruction (exemplified by Chernobyl, nuclear meltdowns were a very real threats during this part of the twentieth century) of the plant she works for, but when neither her lover nor her husband provide a means of sensual and romantic distraction for her, Velma is deeply troubled. Although these sexual relationships had provided great pleasure for the protagonist and these characters channel Yemaya's energy of love sex and sensuality, Velma represents the ways in which Yemaya can be said to defy the very nurturance she is believed to represent. Love, employment, motherhood, and community work function as hindrances to Velma's healing despite the intervention of the spirit world and Minnie Ransom's healing powers. A woman with a cheating husband James Obie Henry and a lover, the local guru Jahmal, Velma seems to be a magnet for trouble. Obie consciously though recognizes this during the time that Velma is falling apart:

> the 7 Arts Academy where both of them work is suffering the same rifting and schisming that Velma is: It was starting up again, [Obie noticed,] the factions, the intrigue. A replay of all the old ideological splits: the street youth as vanguard, the workers as vanguard; self-determination in the Black Belt, Black coalitions, independent political action. Camps were forming to tear the Academy apart . . . He wanted wholeness in his life again. (Bambara 1980, 90)

All Obie could see when looking at Velma is a "crackpot," who is cocooned in a "crusty depression" (Bambara 1980, 100). For Obie "things had seemed more pulled together when Velma had been there, in the house and in the Academy" (Kelley 1993, 484–485). As Velma descends mentally and life falls apart for the character, she represents an expression of Yemoja Ibu Agana, a road associated with madness.

Yemaya's trait of sufferance is often ignored and what many see as the surprising and incomprehensible weeping of Yemaya has perhaps a too-reasonable origin in the Nadir of Black suffering. The beautiful Janie, a romantic at heart, suffers in all three of her marriages. Her husbands, Logan Killicks, Jody Starks, and Tea Cake often mistreat Janie and place her in a subservient role. Hurston contends that Janie's marriages, particularly to Jody, "took all the fight out of Janie's face. For a while she thought it was gone from her soul" (Hurston 1990, 72). Although Jody did not require that Janie engage in manual labor as Logan did, flirtatiously grinning, "A pretty doll-baby lak you is made to sit on de front porch and rock and fan yo'self and eat p'taters dat other folks plant just special for you" (Hurston 1990, 28), he certainly expected Janie to labor in their store and "de home" and to remain quiet: "Joe spoke out without giving her a chance to say anything one way or another that took the bloom off of things" (Hurston 1990, 41). As Jody reveals his domineering side, he further alienates Janie and dampens the burgeoning Yemaya power he had re-awakened,

> The spirit of the marriage left the bedroom and took to living in the parlor . . . So she put something in there to represent the spirit like a Virgin Mary image. The bed was no longer a daisy-field for her and Joe to play in. it was a place where she went and laid down when she was sleepy and tired. She wasn't petal open anymore with him. (Hurston 1990, 67)

Years later in their marriage, to further downplay her still strong intense smoldering sexuality—as his (a much older Jody's) declined—he would slap "Janie until she had a ringing sound in her ears" (Hurston 1990, 67). To further force her to close her petal, Jody would emphasize Janie's age, "You ain't no young pullet no mo'. You'se uh ole hen now" (Hurston 1990, 73) and "You ain't no young girl to be getting' all insulted 'bout yo' looks. You ain no young courtin' gal" (Hurston 1990, 75). Although Janie further withered under Joe Starks' control, having no more "blossomy opening dusting pollen over her man, neither any glistening young fruit where the petals used to be" (Hurston 1990, 68), the townspeople noticed she was a "born orator," and Janie also realizes "Ah knows a few things, and womenfolks thinks sometimes too!" (Hurston 1990, 67). Janie begins to think "about the inside state of her marriage. Time came when she fought back with her tongue as best she could" (Hurston 1990, 68). As the abuse continued and Jody begins to die, "Sorrow dogged by sorrow" weakened Janie's resolve and "She cried often in the weeks that followed" (Hurston 1990, 79).

After Jody's death, Janie removes her headscarf, and realizes her own mature beauty, "She went over to the dresser and looked hard at her skin and features. The young girl was gone, but a handsome woman had taken her place. She tore off the kerchief from her head and let down her plentiful hair" (Hurston 1990, 83). As Janie begins to beautify herself after her pleasure-less slumber from eroticism, we see the reemergence of the less celebrated sensual aspects of Yemaya. After Janie "burnt up every one of her head rags," she decided, "she would have the rest of her life to do as she pleased" (Hurston 1990, 85). Her powerful reassertion opens the way for her romance with her third and youngest husband Tea Cake. Janie began to see the hidden treasure she possessed despite having been "whipped like a cur dog," she'd resolved to continue her great journey for "things." Hurston seems to suggest those *things* are love, but it is also clear "things" refers to self-determination and the wealth of discovery experiences offer—something her grandmother Nanny disallowed, "Nanny belonged to that other kind that loved to deal in scraps" (Hurston 1990, 85). Hurston continues to analogize *things* to "a jewel down inside herself" (Hurston 1990, 85) that Janie wanted to wear and walk around with so "people could see her and gleam it around" (Hurston 1990, 86). Janie's desire to "show her shine" certainly can be interpreted as a characteristic of Yemaya Mayelewo. When she finally meets Tea Cake who "looked like the love thoughts of women" (Hurston 1990, 101), we begin to believe Janie's dreams of love realized. Although her relationship with Tea Cake is a catalyst to her own self-understanding, unfortunately, Janie suffers and experiences immense grief in this relationship as well.

Similarly, Bambara explores this aspect of grief and suffering through Velma's attempt to escape life's tumult. Velma has a support system of women urging her toward wholeness. The Iyami Aje metaphor, represented by the community of women healers and the Seven Sisters, is also intertwined with an aspect of suffering that Yemoja is associated. As a burned-out politi-cal activist, Velma has reached the point of attempting suicide. Velma re-imagines her suicide attempt,

> recalling images of herself in the kitchen with her head in the oven and her wrists slit, she pictures herself as grains of sand sealed in an hourglass: To be that sealed-sound, taste, air, nothing seeping in. To be that unavailable at last, sealed in and the noise of the world, the garbage, locked out. To pour herself grain by grain into the top globe and sift silently down to a heap in the bottom one. That was the sight she'd been on the hunt for . . . And she'd be still in the globes, in the glass jars, sealed from time and life. (Bambara 1980, 19–20)

Velma's failed attempts to unify the diverse elements of her life and her political commitments have ended in a breakdown. Velma's suicide attempt itself is a retreat from disintegration and a withdrawal to a safety. Minnie, the "fabled healer of the district," lovingly petitions the protagonist "[a] re you sure, sweetheart, that you want to be well?" (Bambara 1980, 3) The

community of women assisting Velma on her path to wellness includes her
god-mother Sophie, or "M'Dear," the Seven Sisters Troupe, Jan and Ruby
and the healer Minnie Ransom who herself has a guide or "a sister-advisor,
fleshless, only spirit, full of spunk and spicy wisdom" (Jackson 1982, 52),
Old Wife, as well as small pantheon of female deities and ancestors. As
Minnie's voice drones on, Velma's fractured consciousness allows scenes to
drift in and out—her "soul goes gathering" (Bambara 1980, 57).

> Velma begins to remember, What it's been like being called in on five-minute
> notice after all the interesting decisions had been made, called in out of personal
> loyalty and expected to break her hump pulling off what the men had decided
> was crucial for community good . . . being snatched at by childish, unman-
> nish hands . . . . Like taking on entirely too much: drugs, prisons, alcohol, the
> schools, rape, battered women, abused children . . . the nuclear power issue.
> (Bambara 1980, 58)

Velma does demonstrate Yemaya's all-encompassing fear for the well-being
of her children (Claybourne), but her descent to madness forces Velma to
reassess her role in society and to center her own well-being. The work opens
with Minnie questioning Velma—who is surrounded and perched atop a
stool, like the Aje transformed into a bird—while the radio plays and a litany
by the group, metaphors for the Iyami Aje, murmurs behind her. Velma, with
her multiple lovers and nascent need to fix the hearts of the community's
members most readily represents a melancholy Yemaya Ibu Akinomi who,
"when upset, she can destroy the world." Suicide for Velma was a way to
alleviate herself of the burdens that come with caring for others at the expense
of herself.

In her multitudinous manifestations, Yemaya transgresses heteronormativity, re-genders and un-genders what is articulated as goddess and challenges ideas around femininity and sexuality in ways that do not deny the
significance of Yemaya's performativity of "mother." Otero and Falola con-
tend Yemaya performs a spectrum of genders and possesses an ambiguous
sexuality: "Since Yemaya is noted as a primordial female orisa [*sic*], she is
central to how Yoruba religious discourses enact the power of performing
gender as a reflexive critique and satire of these roles in society and culture"
(Otero and Toyin 2013, xix). Also, through the examination of the aesthetics of Gelede art, Washington shows how Yemaya as one of the Iyami
Aje, "Great Mothers," are often misunderstood as witches; these figures
are instead powerful female spiritual forces that are especially propitiated
during Gelede festival. These selves complicate the most centered aspect of
the deity's avatars true, but by complicating the idea of a natural woman,
through Yemaya rather than Oshun (Erzuli in Hoodoo/Vodou—accessed by

both Bambara and Hurston—who is the Orisha allowed to be sexualized as a coquette—often set up as opposition to Yemoja) I challenge the idea that sex, reproduction and motherhood are "natural" inarguable co-functioning aspects of biological femaleness; thus, the Black female body made *woman* through socially constructed gendered practices, validated via the work of motherhood that we recognize as appropriate for women made true through the spirits we worship is contestable. Indeed, as Butler maintains, the body, even the metaphoric metaphysical body of Orisha, is itself a construction. All bodies then possess a myriad of selves all of whom constitute the domain of the gendered subject's body wherein contradiction, plasticity and dissimilarity are par for the course. By accessing underexplored identities of Yemaya, poet, witch or Aje, warrior, and lover that exists in Lukumí or Santeria cosmology, I do not view these *caminos* as aberrant marginalized identities or as a deviation from the "nature" of Yemaya, but as much a ritualized expression of the diverse discursive performances of femininity as any other. And as Bambara and Hurston destabilize the notion of mother/wife, the deified so-called natural forms of the feminine, through their characters, they enhance our understanding of sexuality and the performativity of gender.

Both works end in the female protagonists surviving, healing, and reuniting with the women with whom they found solace. Hurston's frame narrative concludes with Pheoby and Janie talking, while Bambara's twisting fragmented tale ends with a festival wherein the community of Claybourne attempt to pull together the power of the salt buried in the soil beneath them. The Madonna versus whore/Mammy verses Sapphire tropes are popular polarizing tropes of Black female identity. However, much like Velma and Janie, Yemaya deifies and weaves together these binary constructs superimposed upon her by the dominant society. Manifested in her *caminos*, she defines for herself who she is. Yemaya is a patron saint of a non-essentialist diasporic Black femininity. The diverse personae, aspects, or "roads" that Yemaya manifests allows for a multitudinous analysis of the diversity of women's lives; the ways in which we change, morph and become different; how in different moments in time and space, she becomes both mother and lover and wife and whore. Literary scholars' complication of Black women's erotic identity rejects the problematic whitestream Eurocentric dichotomous archetypes Collins describes that seek to dehumanize and essentialize Black existence. Both Hurston and Bambara's depictions of their female characters are complicated. While both Velma and Janie are nurturing beings, their matronly selves do not singularly define these characters. They instead syncretize their multi-selves and even challenge the prescriptive identities established for them via masculinist whitestream's imposition feminine ideals.

REFERENCES

Bambara, Toni. 1980. *The Salt Eaters*. New York: Random House.

Clark, Mary Ann. 2005. *Where Men Are Wives and Mothers Rule: Santería Ritual Practices and Their Gender Implications*. Gainesville: University of Florida Press.

Collins, Patricia. 2000. *Black Feminist Thought: Knowledge, Consciousness, and the Politics of Empowerment*. New York: Routledge.

Dayan, Joan. 1994. "Erzulie: A Women's History of Haiti." *Research in African Literatures* 25, no. 2: 5–31. www.jstor.org/stable/4618262.

Gates, Henry Lewis. 1990. "Afterword." In *Their Eyes Were Watching God*, edited by Zora Neal Hurston, 185–207. New York: Perennial Library.

Gonzalez-Wippler, Migene. 1989. *Santeria, the Religion: A Legacy of Faith, Rites and Magic*. New York: Harmony Books.

Hurston, Zora Neal. 1990. *Their Eyes Were Watching God*. New York: Perennial Library.

Hurston, Zora Neal. 2008. *Tell My Horse: Ifa and Life in Haiti and Jamaica*. New York: Harper Perennial.

Jackson, Angela. 1982. "Review *the Salt Eaters* by Toni Cade Bambara." *The Black Scholar* 13, no. 6: 52.

Kelley, Margot Anne. 1993. "'Damballah Is the First Law of Thermodynamics': Modes of Access to Toni Cade Bambara's *The Salt Eaters*." *African American Review* 27, no. 2 (Month/Season): 479–493.

Lawal, Babtunde. 1996. *The Gelede Spectacle: Art, Gender, and Social Harmony in an African Culture*. Seattle: University of Washington Press.

Lee, Shayne. 2010. *Erotic Revolutionaries: Black Women, Sexuality, and Popular Culture*. Lahnam: Hamilton Books.

Logan, Rayford Whittingham. 1987. *The Betrayal of the Negro, from Rutherford B. Hayes to Woodrow Wilson*. Boston: Da Capo Press.

Matory, J. Lorand. 2005. "Oriki Yemoja (Yemoja Panegyrics)." In *Sex and the Empire That Is No More: Gender and the Politics of Metaphor in Oyo Yoruba Religion*. New York: Berghahn Books.

Montgomery, Eric James. 2016. "Syncretism in Vodu and Orisha an Anthropological Analysis." *Journal of Religion and Society* 18: 1–22.

Omi, Olo. 2009. *Pataki of Orisa and Other Essays for Lucumi Santeria Vol. 1*. Morrisville, NC: Lulu.com.

Otero, Solimar, and Toyin Falola. 2013. Introduction to *Yemoja: Gender, Sexuality, and Creativity in the Latina/o and Afro-Atlantic Diasporas*, edited by Solimar Otero and Toyin Falola, xxi. New York: State University of New York Press.

Pérez, Elizabeth. 2013. "Nobody's Mammy: Yemaya as Fierce Foremother in Afro-Cuban Religions." In *Yemoja: Gender, Sexuality, and Creativity in the Latina/o and Afro-Atlantic Diasporas*, edited by Solimar Otero and Toyin Falola, 9–43. New York: State University of New York Press.

Saide, Omi. 2018. Interview by Khalilah Ali. April 7, 2018.

Washington Teresa, N. ed. 2005. "Aje Across the Continent and in Itankale." In *Our Mothers, Our Powers, Our Texts: Manifestations of Ajé in Africana Literature*. Bloomington: Indiana University Press.

Weir-Soley, Donna. 2009. "Literary Interventions in Their Eyes Were Watching God." In *Eroticism, Spirituality, and Resistance in Black Women's Writings*, 39–78. Gainesville: University Press of Florida.

Chapter 9

"A Small Piece of Blue Fabric"

*Manifestations of Yemonja as a
Site of Generational Healing in
Phyllis Alesia Perry's* Stigmata

Griselda Thomas

In 1998, Phyllis Alesia Perry emerged with her first novel *Stigmata* that clearly draws from her contemporary literary foremothers, such as Toni Morrison, Alice Walker, and Octavia Butler. Like these writers, and others, Perry uses fiction to explore cross-generational trauma and healing by connecting her Black female protagonist, Elizabeth Joyce "Lizzie" DuBose, to her ancestors. More specifically, Perry employs family heirlooms and incarnations from the past to tell a story of ancestral trauma caused by the transAtlantic slave trade, generational survival, and relational healing. In this chapter, I explore the manifestations of the Yoruba deity, Yemonja, by examining, what I refer to as, Lizzie's transmigrations through time and space, and the role of the quilt bequeathed to her by her maternal grandmother, Grace. To accomplish this, I rely on transmigration as a literary device and the literary quilt trope to explicate reclamation and recognition of Yemonja, the Yoruba orisha associated with motherhood and the feminine divine, in *Stigmata*.

TRANSMIGRATION AS A LITERARY DEVICE

Transmigration, as a literary device, acknowledges the spiritual, social, and historical significance of the actual physical movement of "the Black body" through time and space. I use the term in my analysis of *Stigmata* to explore the characteristics of spiritual and physical incarnations that involve the semiokinetic movement of Lizzie through time and space. Instead of using the more general concept reincarnation, transmigration expands the discussion of

99

incarnation to one about the presence of African spiritually, more specifically Yemonja, in Perry's novel. Moreover, transmigration goes beyond the spiritual migration of the characters in the novel and evokes images of the forced migration of Africans to America, as well as their great migrations from the south to the north. The term is critical to an understanding of the African American experience, the trauma of displacement, and the significance of Yemonja in the lives of Africans in its diaspora. Similar to "spirituality as ideology" proposed by Judylyn S. Ryan in her book *Spirituality as Ideology in Black Women's Film and Literature*, spiritual transmigration "illustrates the centrality of spirituality to Black visions of transformation" and "charts the dual engagement with spirituality as an aspect of intertextual relations among Black women artist of the diaspora" writing about the diaspora (Ryan 2005, 7–8).

In *Stigmata*, the protagonist Lizzie is the incarnation of her great-great-grandmother Ayo, a survivor of the Middle Passage and chattel slavery in Alabama, and her grandmother Grace who mysteriously disappears from the lives of her children, one of whom is Sarah, Lizzie's mother. However, these women do not only live in Lizzie, but there are times that they seem to exist alongside her. In many ways, the past permeates Lizzie's life. In her transmigration, she relives the horrible experiences of Ayo and Grace, which stretch back over 150 years. However, unlike Edana "Dana" Franklin, the protagonist in Octavia Butler's *Kindred* who physically travels back and forth in time and actually endures the brutality of enslavement as a result her own actions, Lizzie physically remains in the present while she endures the brutality that Ayo suffered during the Middle Passage. Dana bears the scars from her experience in the past; Lizzie bears the scars from her great-great-grandmother Ayo's experience in the past. Dana must make "dizzying" trips to the past as a part of her transmigration through time and space while Lizzie experiences many of her transmigrations by simply wrapping herself in her grandmother Grace's quilt in the present.

THE QUILT AS A LITERARY TROPE

The story quilt plays a major role in the transmigration and relational healing that take place in *Stigmata*. Along with being the impetus of Lizzie's transmigration, it is also the site of spiritual understanding and confirmation for Lizzie as well as emotional and psychological healing for Lizzie, Grace, and Sarah. In many ways, the role of the quilt in the lives of the women in *Stigmata* parallels the history of the quilt in the lives of African American women overall. But this history is not so much political or social history as it is spiritual and personal history. The discovery of the coded patchwork quilts that enslaved women made to help those seeking freedom find their way on the Underground Railroad fills in one of many gaps in the history of ordinary enslaved women and the role they played as revolutionary artists and activists in their efforts to assist Black people out of bondage. A gap in the history of ordinary enslaved women is how they survived the Middle Passage. Of this experience and the African people forced to endure it, Toni Morrison says in a filmed interview, "nobody knows their names, and nobody thinks of them. In addition to that, they never survived in the lore, there are no songs or dances or tales about these people. The people who arrived, there is lore about them. But nothing survives about – that" ("Toni Morrison"), referring to the Middle Passage. *Stigmata* brings attention to that "that" when Ayo tells Joy to record in her diary (also bequeathed to Lizzie), *"I am Ayo. Joy. I choose to remember. This is for those whose bones lie in the heart of mother ocean for those who tomorrows I never knew who groaned and died in the damp dark beside me. You rite this daughter for me and for them* [emphasis original]" (Perry 1998, 7).

Yemonja is often referred as the river or the one who possess the "life-giving properties of the river" (Wippler 1972, 100). In *Our Mothers, Our Powers, Our Texts: Manifestations of Aje in Africana Literature,* Teresa Washington writes, "the Mother [who] enslaved Africans first thanked for surviving the Middle Passage of death was Yemoja: No matter what immediate atrocities life held, the external covenant of Mothers of Waters—of peace, evolution, and rebirth—would not be broken" (Washington 2005, 236). Yemonja is the orisha that African people in the Americas praise as responsible for their ancestors' survival of the Middle Passage, and therefore, their existence. She is also the deity who looks after their ancestors who did not survive the death voyage to the Americas.

Subsequently, Ayo's diary becomes the key to Lizzie's understanding of the quilt that records her transmigration. Without Ayo's dairy, Grace's quilt simply represents a story cloaked in cloth. Ayo, like all of the enslaved women who found themselves suddenly members of a free and hostile patriarchal white supremacist society, understands the importance of preserving her story. It is not to say that she does not value her lineage as the daughter of a "fabric griot" (textile dyer), for she also honors this tradition. Of the evening of Ayo's death, Joy writes in Ayo's diary that her mother took her hand, placed it on the baby's quilt and said, *"Take care of that little girl she say and she smiled and say I meant to put this in but I never did and she gave me a piece of blue cloth she had balled up in her hand* [emphasis original]*"* (Perry 1998, 230). The baby girl that Ayo is referring to is Grace. The blue cloth that Ayo is referring to is from the dress she was wearing when slave catchers stole her from Africa. Grace's life begins where Ayo's ends, and the small piece of blue cloth becomes central to the survival of another generation.

Although the novel centers on Lizzie's transmigrations, Grace's transmigrations are the ones recorded on the story quilt bequeathed to Lizzie. With no way to understand and explain the transmigrations that forced her to leave her family, Grace makes the quilt as a way to piece together the episodes she is experiencing during her transmigrations. Therefore, Grace's quilt is not only the impetus for Lizzie's transmigration but also the medium through which Grace will come to learn of her legacy as one of the forever people and understand her transmigration. In her letter to her sister Mary Nell, Grace writes that she finished and sent the quilt she was working on before she left Johnson Creek: "It's finished and Ayo's whole story is set on it. I feel better now it's through . . . I thought getting it all down on the quilt in front of me out of me would get rid of it somehow." In the same letter, Grace also tells Mary Nell, "I feel that others after us will need to know. Our grands maybe will need to get these things. Please leave these for my granddaughter. I know she aint here yet. But I have faith that you and Eva will know when the time is right and when it is she will be waiting" (Perry 1998, 15). Grace trusts Mary Nell and Eva to know when the time is right because they are psychic or what John Mbiti defines as *seers*: "people who are said to have natural power by means of which they 'see' certain things not easily known to other people. Sometimes they foresee events before they take place . . . They are often people with a sharp capacity for both foresight and insight into things" (Mbiti 1998, 159). It is because of this gift that Mary Nell and Eva know which one of Grace's two granddaughters should inherit the trunk. They also know when it is time to give the trunk to Lizzie, which is after the death of Mary Nell. After her great-aunt's funeral, Lizzie returns to Tuskegee with her parents and the trunk whose content include the quilt and a small piece of blue cloth.

The night Lizzie first brings the quilt home from her Johnson Creek relatives' house, Lizzie and Sarah are equally intrigued about what is in the trunk. However, there is tension between Sarah and the quilt. Sarah is the first one to actually spread the quilt out and look at it. In her close studying of the quilt, she does see the appliqué of a child wearing a dress the color of one she used to have. Sarah takes a deep breath and questions the type of quilt that Grace has started. She only sees "pictures stuck to a background" with "no rhyme or reason." Yet Grace has written about them in her letter as if they mean something. Despite recognizing the piece of fabric from the dress she once wore, Sarah does not see a clear connection between herself and the quilt. Perhaps, she is disconnected from the quilt Grace made because she needs to repress the memory of Grace's (her mother's) suddenly leaving her as a young child. Sarah's middle-class eye will not allow her to see beauty in the quilt, a result of the middle-class life she escaped to long ago to avoid the pain caused by her mother's abandonment of her. In any case, Sarah appears disconnected from and distressed by the quilt while Lizzie immediately recognizes that the quilt has meaning. When Lizzie explains the story to Sarah, she sees her mother smile at her with her mouth only. The absence of light in Sarah's eyes makes Lizzie feel she is causing her mother pain that she is unable to stop. Lizzie is able to see what her mother is not able to see, and she feels that by knowing, she is hurting her mother. Sarah is not in the generation of transmigration, and thus will need help before she is comfortable with the quilt and the story that has been sewn onto it.

Lizzie, fascinated by the quilt right away, seems to have a special love for it, and always wants to wrap herself in it. The quilt is an appliqué quilt and the first thing we learn about the story it depicts is that there are two figures, a brown woman and a child walking down the roadside by side with baskets on their heads. The night after she opens the trunk for the first time, Lizzie puts the quilt to "everyday use" and falls asleep under it. Lizzie remarks that as she lays in her twin-sized bed, she feels encapsulated by the quilt, protected and secure. For Lizzie, the quilt she covers herself in is not only a blanket of protection but a material object that tells the story of her own life. Lizzie feels connected to the brown woman who is sewn into the quilt, so connected that when she covers herself in the quilt by pulling it over her head, "the twilight world of dreams" arrives. This dream portal, facilitated by Lizzie and her quilt can be read as an intergenerational connection, too. One could say that Lizzie is experiencing "an elaborate fantasy about her ancestors" (Perry 1998, 137–138), which is the diagnosis of the first psychiatrist to whom she will later be sent, but at this point in the story, Lizzie has never heard of Ayo. One could say that she is experiencing what critics have termed "rememory," but this is a memory of an experience that she has never had, of a story she has never heard, and of a place she has never seen. One could say that Lizzie is dreaming. However, when she "wake[s] to bright Alabama day, there is dust about [her] feet" that is not of the Alabama soil (Perry 1998, 25). Like Dana in Butler's *Kindred*, Lizzie has physically moved through space and time, as evidenced by the dust on her feet, and transmigrated to a previous life. Lizzie's transmigrations will become more painful and disturbing, and the experience of transmigration will become a devastating mystery to Lizzie and will remain so until she is able to recognize that the story in the quilt is her own story.

The transmigration that causes Lizzie to be institutionalized is one in which she experiences a great deal of bleeding from Ayo's shackles. There is so much blood that it flowed onto the quilt, and then the carpet. When Lizzie wakes up screaming from the "raw unapologetic pain" (Perry 1998, 146), her middle-class parents living in suburbia in 1980 rush into her room to find her bleeding from her wrists. Thinking it is a suicide attempt, they call the paramedics, and Lizzie is taken to the hospital.

A lot of the deciphering of the quilt takes place during the fourteen years Lizzie spends in psychiatric hospitals, repeatedly transmigrating into Ayo's and Grace's lives until she knows the stories of their lives. Lizzie will learn to feign sanity so that she can be released from her imprisonment, but when she is released she still doesn't understand everything. She doesn't understand why she had to go through her ordeal. It is only when she goes back to the quilt that she begins to gain understanding and healing.

The first thing that Lizzie must learn is how to readjust her worldview. Despite the transmigrations she has already experienced, she is still a product of post–civil rights Black middle-class intellectualization and rationalization, which does not allow her to connect completely to her African past or to understand the story in the quilt. During her first visit with Dr. Daniels, prior to the transmigration that lands her in an institution, Lizzie is at a loss for words when she tries to explain to the doctor what she is experiencing. Of course Dr. Daniels thinks that her explanations for the scars that circle her wrist are "elaborate fantasies about her ancestor," "old stories," and "glorified dreams" (Perry 1998, 137–138). And Lizzie, herself, seems unable to move beyond similar explanations when she first describes what is happening. Even at the end of the fourteen years, when Lizzie has learned a great deal about Ayo and Grace, she has not fully understood the significance of her transmigration. She leaves the institution believing she is mentally unstable, but that she has learned to manipulate the doctors by pretending to be sane (Perry 1998, 6).

When Lizzie is finally released from the last of the many institutions she lived in, she returns to Johnson Creek to retrieve the quilt. She now studies the quilt in a way that she had not done before because she realizes, as Eva had told her years before, that Grace's quilt, along with Ayo's diary, are the keys that will unlock the door to the past. It is obvious that Lizzie has unlocked that door and through her transmigrations entered the past. Now she must figure out what to do with that past, which she contemplates further by revisiting Grace's quilt.

AFRICAN-CENTERED THEORY AS EXPLANATION

Quilts and quilting are so prominently linked to transmigration in this novel that it makes sense to look here at Afrocentric scholar Marimba Ani's discussion of the link between the material and the spiritual in her monograph, *Let the Circle Be Unbroken: The Implications of Spirituality in the Diaspora.* Ani often writes about "Africa" as a unified whole. She also sees Africans and African Americans as one people. Ani does not tease out the differences or contradictions among and between different religions, philosophies, and cultures in Africa and the Diaspora; instead, she looks for commonalities and then compares these African commonalities to certain Western commonalities in an attempt to distinguish "African" culture from Western culture. Ani does not seem to see a need to justify defining "Africa" so broadly, but she does stress that she is primarily concerned with addressing "what happens when a people are forced to live (survive) within a culture based on a worldview that is oppressive to their ethos" (Ani 1980, 4).

Defining "African" and "Western" in these broad ways, Ani writes about how the African "ethos" and "worldview" are different from the Western/European ethos and worldview and how each set of ethos and worldview sees spirituality and matter. Ani defines "ethos" as "the emotional substance of a cultural group . . . their collective emotional tone." Describing African ethos, she writes "Our spirit symbolizes our uniqueness as a people, or we could say that the African-American ethos is spiritual." She defines "worldview" as the thing that "injects meaning into life." Worldview includes "conceptions of the structure of the universe, the relationship and origin of nature and human beings, truth and knowledge, reality and the nature of being." She sees both ethos and wordview as making up "culture" which is collective, "not created individually" (Ani 1980, 3).

Ani believes that the concept of dualism is distinctly Western; in this system, realities are separated into opposing pairs with one member of each pair valued over the other. In this system, the spiritual and the material are often viewed as one such pair. The spiritual is the higher or more valued member of this pair, and as such, it must be used to control the material.

By contrast, Ani says that in the African worldview, "the universe is made up of complementary pairs" (Ani 1980, 6). These "pairs are forces, or principles of reality that are interdependent and necessary to each other, in a unified system" (Ani 1980, 6). Discussing spirituality and materiality in this light, Ani explains that spirit and matter interrelate in "harmonious interaction." Deities and ancestors together possess the spiritual power to strengthen the life force of the people, and these deities and ancestors depend on the sacrifices (usually made of physical matter) of living people in order to strengthen their own spiritual power. In this way, "the spirits 'need' us, just as we 'need' them; just as spirit 'needs' matter to give it form, and matter 'needs' spirit to give it force, being and reality" (Ani 1980, 7).

Within her discussion of the material and spiritual significance of ancestors, Ani also writes about family. She writes:

Life, events, and phenomena derive meaning, value or significance through relationship to an organic whole. The family or community is understood as just such a "whole." And since nothing of significance is merely physical the community itself becomes a metaphysical reality. We say that the African family includes the "dead," "the living," and the "yet unborn." Its significance is multi-dimensional, and it is through Ancestor Communion that its wholeness gives meaning and definition to the family members.

Spiritual realities are timeless; that is, they are not limited by ordinary categories of time and space. Through its association with spirit, matter becomes ontologically related to the eternal. (Ani 1980, 7)

If we read *Stigmata* through the lens of Ani's understanding of spirit, matter, ancestors, and family, we might see the various quilts made by Ayo, Grace, Lizzie, and Sarah as comprising the "matter" that strengthens spiritual power, especially if we define Grace's and Lizzie's transmigrations as spiritually powerful.

Moreover, if we think of Lizzie's family in terms of Ani's definition of the African family, it is easy to see the multidimensionality that Ani is referring to in her discussion about the material and spiritual significance of ancestors. If, as Ani suggests, "it is through Ancestor Communion that [the African family's] wholeness gives meaning and definition to the family members," then Grace's communion with Ayo and Lizzie's communion with Ayo and Grace take on new meaning. This family definitely "includes the 'dead,' 'the living,' and the 'yet unborn'" (Perry 1998, 7).

Ani explains that "much of African religious activity . . . involves the attempt to strengthen [the] force vitale of 'life force'" because the thing most highly valued in the African worldview is living energetically and forcefully. In the Yoruba religion, this life force was called *magara*. According to Janheinz Jahn in *Muntu: African Culture and the Western World*, *magara* is "expressed in the living human being in contentment and happiness" (Jahn 1990, 111). It increases in people who are living through the influence of their dead ancestors, but the flow of *magara* is not one-way. The living are also able to strengthen their dead ancestors (Jahn 1990, 111). As a Middle Passage survivor who lived her life in chattel slavery, Ayo's *magara* is interrupted. The legacy of slavery thwarts this force in the lives of Ayo's female descendants as well: Joy must transcribe Ayo's life even as much of it remains unspeakable; Grace must relive and bear the physical and emotional consequences of the horrific events of Ayo's life; Lizzie's pain is multiplied as she must live both Ayo's and Grace's pain; and Sarah, whom Lisa A. Long describes, in her article "A Relative Pain: The Rape of History in Octavia Butler's *Kindred* and Phyllis Alesia Perry's *Stigmata*" as "perhaps the most damaged character in *Stigmata*" (Long 2002, 473), must lose both her mother and her daughter as she avoids and struggles to understand the transmigration(s). *Magara* is needed in the lives of these women. Jahn writes that "the departed are spiritual forces which can influence their living descendants. In this, their only purpose is to increase the life force of their descendants." He also explains, "a dead person can be born again in several different individuals, for example in his grandchildren" (Jahn 1990, 111).

If Ayo's spirit seeks, as its "only purpose," to increase the magara of Ayo's descendants and their relationship with their ancestors, it certainly does not have a simple task. Perhaps this is why it takes a few generations of transmigration for the magara to start flowing again. Marimba Ani explains that in African philosophy, the health of the family is directly dependent upon the family's daily communion with their ancestors through ritual. Ritual expresses "interrelationship with other beings in the universe" and "it is through ritual that the unexplainable is 'understood.'" Ani goes on to explain that

> Universally, in ritual the African combines life with artistic expression. Ritual is, in a sense, the ultimate philosophical expression of the African world-view, for it is the modality within which the unity of the human and the divine is expressed, in which the unity of spirit and matter is perceived, and in which Eternal Moment is achieved. When we perform rituals as our ancestors did, *we become our ancestors*, and so transcend the boundaries of ordinary space and time, and the limitations of separation they impose. (emphasis mine) (Ani 1980, 8–9)

In much the same way that the quilts in *Stigmata* can be thought of as the "matter" that complements the spirit, the act of quilting can be thought of as a kind of ritual.

Quilting is not new to this family of women. Eva and Mary Nell are also quilters, but Grace was more skilled than her sisters. Ayo's mother, like Yemonja, according to John Mason, was a fabric dyer in Africa; Grace's baby quilt was made by Ayo; and Ayo's story quilt, which was also Lizzie's transmigration quilt, was made by Grace (Mason 1992, 311). Grace bequeathed that quilt to Lizzie, and Lizzie and Sarah make a story quilt about Grace's life. Not only do all of these women quilt, but they teach each other to quilt, they quilt together, and they give quilts to each other. Perry uses the quilt as a metaphor for the fragmentation in these women's lives, but also as a metaphor for their interconnectedness. Generations share stories around the quilt as they quilt together and teach each other to quilt. Ayo begins the recitation of her life while cutting quilt pieces, and she gives Joy a baby quilt she has made for the not-yet-born Grace the day she dies.

In her essay, "Kinship and Quilting: An Examination of an African-American Tradition," Africana Studies scholar Floris Barnett Cash discusses the prominent role quilting has played in connecting generations and communities of Black women. She writes, "African-American women, whose voices are largely unknown, have often unconsciously created their own lives and are the voices of authority on their experiences. The voices of black women are stitched within their quilts" (Cash 1995, 36). Cash provides examples of the importance of quilting throughout generations of African American women. During enslavement, quilts were sometimes used to purchase the freedom of the quilter or her loved ones, quilting bees were sites of resistance in the civil rights movement and the Women's Movement, and for generations, quilting was (and sometimes still is) a source of networking, especially in rural areas. According to Cash, one of the most salient aspects of the common cultural heritage of AfricanAmerican women is the importance of kinship. She explains:

> Kinship networks for African-American women have existed across generations among slave women, tenant farm wives, middle-class women, and senior citizens, thus empowering them with self-help and self-esteem. Kin and family arrangements of enslaved Africans emerge from the social and cultural processes which transform them into African-Americans. Through kinship they stabilized family relationships. Kinship networks formed the foundation for a new African-American culture. The slave community functioned as an extended kinship system. Black women carried these concepts of mutual assistance with them from bondage to freedom.
>
> For African-American women, the basis of family structure and cooperation was an extended family of kinship ties, blood relations and non-kin as well. Female networks promoted self-reliance and self-help. They sustained hope and provided survival strategies. (Cash 1995, 31)

The kind of ancestor communion that Marimba Ani believes is necessary for *magara* to flow freely in the lives of African peoples is accomplished in *Stigmata* largely through the quilts and the ritual of quilting in the lives of Ayo, Grace, and Lizzie.

A SMALL PIECE OF BLUE FABRIC

One of the most obvious "connecting threads" in the quilts of these women is a particular piece of fabric. It is fabric dyed by Ayo in Africa and made into the dress Ayo is wearing the day she is captured by slavers. Before transferring to the slave ship, Ayo's captors rip the dress from her body, but Ayo manages to grab the dress and a piece of it tears off in her hand. She clutches the cloth in her fist throughout the Middle Passage, and she holds it again on the auction block. This piece of blue fabric is the most tangible evidence of Ayo's lineage in Africa, and the thread that connects five generations of women together as it migrates from woman to woman and from quilt to quilt.

The color blue in African textiles carries strong spiritual connotations. The Yoruba considered blue a spiritual color (Tobin and Dobard 1999, 50). Among the Yoruba orisa, Yemonja, the "ultimate symbol and the personification of motherhood" who wears seven skirts of blue and white, is one of the most powerful (Mason 1992, 307). She is the deity of the Ogun river, the largest river in ancient Yoruba, which was considered by the ancient people of the Ifa religion to be the birthplace of all life on earth. Later, as these same people were forced into slavery in the Americas through the Middle Passage and the Yoruba became familiar with the ocean, Yemonja's became Yemaya and her domain expanded. Although her symbol changed from river to the top layer of the sea, she remained the mother of all life (Mason 1992, 307). It is interesting to consider Yemonja in this discussion of the "blue" in *Stigmata*, because she was thought to have kept alive the survivors of the Middle Passage. Perry doesn't tell us whether Ayo and her mother lived in Nigeria or whether they practiced the Ifa religion, but if we imagine that they did, we might also imagine that some of the blue cloth Ayo's mother dyed was used to make the skirts worn by worshippers of Yemonja. If Ayo's mother had known what happened to Ayo the day she wandered off, she likely would have been relieved to remember that Ayo was wearing a dress made of her blue cloth, and she might have hoped that Ayo would be able to take a piece of it with her. She probably would have attributed Ayo's survival to Yemonja's protection, and she might have seen the blue cloth as a symbol of Yemonja.

Once in the Americas, people who worshipped Yemonja came to believe that she manifests herself in certain characteristics of her worshippers. These characteristics included strength, willfulness, forgiveness, and domesticity. And because quilting and domesticity go hand in hand, we might see Yemonja's presence in the quilting done by Ayo, Grace, and Lizzie, all of whom are unrelenting and determined to protect their family and preserve their legacy as forever people.

The spiritual significance of the color blue manifests itself in various forms of folk material. Throughout the Americas, glass bottle trees, which can be traced to the Kongo and Angola, have been made to catch roaming spirits that might be harmful to a person's home or well-being. Blue was the preferred color of bottles used for trapping misdirected spirits for these bottle trees (Thompson 1984, 142; Tobin and Dobbard 1992, 50). In the same way that the blue bottles trapped the roaming spirits, the blue cloth can be seen as trapping the lost souls of the Middle Passage. And in the same way that the bottles on the bottle tree seem to serve a dual purpose, the blue cloth in *Stigmata* serves a similar dual purpose. The bottles of the tree not only trap souls that are roaming (thus giving them a home) but also serve to protect the residents of the home by protecting their house from those same souls (trapped in the bottles to keep them from doing mischief) as well as from thieves who avoid the house out of fear of the souls in the bottles. Similarly, the piece of blue fabric held in Ayo's hand and passed on through five generations of women serves a dual purpose. It provides a home for the roaming soul of Ayo's suffering, or perhaps for the roaming souls of those who died next to Ayo on the slave ship. It also protects these women by providing a connecting thread that will ultimately facilitate their understanding and begin to heal them. It also becomes a tool in terms of holding those spirits just as the bottles in bottle trees hold roaming spirits. Ayo's experience is so intense that her spirit continues to roam. This is the spirit of the forever people. This particular piece of blue fabric has trauma in it, having been ripped off of Ayo's body and having been held in her hand during the Middle Passage. Thus it carries a powerful symbolism as the manifestation of Yemonja becomes a major motif in the novel.

The enslaved women on Ibo Island in Julie Dash's film *Daughters of the Dust* are indigo fabric dyers who make the indigo dye in a huge iron pot. In the film, the hands of these women appear to be forever stained a deep blue. In her examination of Dash's moving presentation of the Peazant family, Judylyn S. Ryan suggests that "In Dash's moving presentation of the Peazant family, the recurring image of Black hands 'scarred blue with the poisonous indigo dye that built up all those plantations from swampland' becomes a visual code for the history of Slavery that informs all situations and events in the present" (Ryan 2005, 36). In reality, the hands of indigo dyers are not permanently stained in such an extreme manner. In her book *Daughters of the Dust: The Making of an African American Woman's Film*, Julie Dash says she uses this image "as a symbol of slavery, to create a new kind of icon around slavery rather than the traditional showing of the whip marks or the chains . . . we've seen all those things before and we've become very calloused about them. I wanted to show it in a new way" (Dash 1992, 31). According to Ryan, "although slavery is not the explicit subject of the film, its shadow lurks in the stor[ies]" of the Peazant women (Ryan 2005, 36). In the same way, the blue in Ayo's hand—the blue piece of cloth that Ayo brings to America balled up in her fist—becomes a powerful symbol, a shadow representing Ayo's capture, Middle Passage and enslavement, a shadow that lurks in the lives of Joy, Grace, Sarah, and Lizzie.

Perry makes the holding of the cloth in a hand important by creating a sequence of similar "holdings" throughout the novel. Ayo first remembers that as she was being stripped for the passage to America, "They tore the cloth from my body that day by the sea facing west, but I held on, held on to something, balled it in my fist forever" (Perry 1998, 47). Just as she held the cloth during the Middle Passage, she holds it again on the auction block: "I remember my fist being closed tight for what seem like years . . . I had a piece of cloth balled up in there. Beautiful blue cloth. But what I was wearin was just brown" (Perry 1998, 133). For Ayo, the small piece of blue cloth represents more than the traumatic experience that she endured. With the tattered piece of cloth, Perry, like Dash, creates another visual code of the slavery, which connects Black women's manual and creative work. When we imagine the beautiful garments that were made from the indigo cloth created by indigo-stained hands of enslaved women, we are also reminded of the quilts that enslaved women made for their mistresses who took full credit for their creation. But, unlike Dash, Perry's code has a dual purpose. The blue cloth establishes a link from Africa through slavery and into the twentieth century by transferring the trauma into pieces of art that are for the family's everyday use. Thus it becomes the center of a medium (the quilt) that each generation can build upon and link back to the past. And, as Lizzie explains to Eva (who already knows), "The past—that's what you call it—is a circle. If you walk long enough, you catch up with yourself" (Perry 1998, 117). In *Stigmata,* then, the African spirit is in the blue cloth which centers Grace's and Lizzie's lives during their transmigrations. With their understanding of the past that is represented in the cloth, the African spirit moves across time to enable the protagonists to achieve these deeper, spiritual consciousness.

LET THE CIRCLE BE UNBROKEN

The circle is one of the earliest symbols utilized by ancient African civilizations, representing infinity and the regeneration of life. In his book *Slave Culture: Nationalist Theory and the Foundation of Black America*, Sterling Stuckey describes the circle's association to such symbols that are so vital to life and spirituality among various ethnic groups throughout Africa. He says:

> An integral part of religion and culture was movement in a ring during ceremonies honoring the ancestors. There is, in fact, substantial evidence for the importance of the ancestral function of the circle in West Africa, but the circle ritual imported by Africans from the Congo region was so powerful in its elaboration of a religious vision that it contributed disproportionately to the centrality of the circle in slavery. The use of the circle for religious purposes in slavery was so consistent and profound that one could argue that it was what gave form and meaning to black religion and art. (Stuckey 1987, 11)

We can see in *Stigmata* a series of connections and circles linking spirituality and ancestry to the ritual of quilt making. Ani contends that "African life is replete with ritual," which as Stuckey explains often takes place in a circle (Stuckey 1987, 8). The ceremonial circle also involves connecting the present (the living) to the past (the dead/ancestors). Ayo and Grace use the ritual of quilting to connect their lives with the lives of their children and their children's children (born and unborn). Lizzie uses the ritual of quilting to bond with Sarah, who is both her mother and her daughter. In different ways both Lizzie and Grace use the ritual of quilting to understand and explain their transmigrations. All of this is done to create continuity from one generation to the next.

The movement of the circle begins when Ayo tells her daughter Joy to "rite" in the diary, *"My name mean happiness she say. Joy. That why I name you that so I don't forget who I am and what I mean to the world* [emphasis original]" (Perry 1998, 7). Ayo was given the slave name Bessie when she arrived in America. She reconnects with her African past by re-naming herself Ayo in the first entry of the diary she will keep with Joy. This act is, in some ways, characteristic of naming ceremonies that are held in many African societies. Not only do the ceremonies celebrate the birth of a child, but they also acknowledge the significance of the child's birth, which is denoted by the given name. The ritualistic keeping of the diary that Ayo initiates connects her to her daughter and begins the loop back to the past and the forever people who live "at the bottom of heaven . . . in the circle" by making known her African identity among her progeny (Perry 1998, 7).

Ayo moves the circle into the next generation when she makes a quilt for her unborn granddaughter, Grace. She explains to Joy, *"She cant get here cause Im in the way she say. But when Im gone she come to take my place. She gon know thangs the one thats comin. She'll know things and that knowin be a gift from me her family that's lost.* [emphasis original]" The baby quilt that Ayo gives Grace does not include Ayo's story, for she knows that Grace will know things. Ayo is certain to provide Grace with all the things (the piece of blue cloth and the diary) she needs to understand the "gift" that will cause her emotional and physical pain. The small piece of blue cloth and the diary will also help Grace to translate the story of the forever people to the quilt, thereby keeping the circle moving (Perry 1998, 34).

Grace's gift comes in the form of her transmigrations. She makes a quilt on which to record the people in her transmigrations and the family she left behind so that she will not forget. In telling the story of the pain she endured as a result of leaving her family and enduring her transmigration, Grace's quilt becomes as Lizzie calls it, her "mourning cloth" and she finds understanding and closure by making it. As Ani writes, "It is through ritual that the unexplainable is 'understood,' that chaos is made to be ordered within the logic of tradition" (Ani 1997, 8).

What is most interesting about the quilt that Grace makes is the fact that it is an appliqué quilt. It is the same type that Harriet Powers made by merging African appliqué techniques with her use of symbols rooted in West African, Central African, and Haitian culture along with European record keeping and biblical reference traditions (Wahlman 2001, 65). In a similar fashion, Grace merges the textile tradition of the unnamed brown woman, Ayo's mother, and Ayo's dairy to create a spiritual medium by which to keep a record of the forever people. This quilt is different from the patchwork quilts that Grace and her family traditionally made. Her choice of a new quilt style shows her attempt to evoke change while continuing the circle that Ayo started.

Lizzie becomes the bearer of eternity when she transmigrates as a result of physically engaging Grace's quilt. Although this quilt brings closure to Grace, it will open up a Pandora's box for Lizzie. Lizzie will also find closure and continue the circle when she decides to tell "Grace's story with this quilt—just as [Grace] had told Ayo's story with hers—and the fabric has to hold up at least until the next storyteller comes along" (Perry 1998, 63). Like the quilt that Grace made, Lizzie's quilt will also be an appliqué quilt—a story quilt. The appliqué quilt is the preferred genre of many contemporary quilt makers because its form encourages the "celebrating of oral history through fabric" (Tobin and Dobard 1999, 155). These modern day "fabric griots" consciously evoke the past, mend the present, and shape the future with their stories on cloth. Lizzie wants to continue the legacy without the pain.

Lizzie makes her story quilt to fill in the gaps represented by the generations—Joy, Mary Nell, Eva, Sarah, and Ruth—who are not forever people. However, Joy was brought into the circle when she "rites" Ayo's diary for her. Mary Nell, Eva, and, to some degree, Ruth were able to enter the circle because they are blessed with the ability to see what others cannot see. But Sarah, unlike Mary Nell—"a smiling spirit"—Eva "with her clairvoyant stuff," and Ruth "a kindred spirit," is unable to recognize the legacy of eternity that Ayo has bestowed on her descendants.

Sarah is outside the circle and cannot imagine the world the way her relatives see it.

For Sarah, the past and the transmigrations of Grace and Lizzie (her mother/daughter) represent emotional and internal pain. Lizzie feels that she can bring Sarah into the circle through the ritual of quilting. She believes that if she can get Sarah to fully participate in making a quilt about Grace's life, Sarah will finally understand why her mother had to leave her, and will thus begin to heal from the emotional pain that has cut her off from the circle. For several months, Lizzie purposely lives at home, making it her mission to involve her mother in every aspect of the quilt. Lizzie tells Sarah that the quilt is a personification of the past, a past that they can re-remember and also move through. Although Sarah has a difficult time comprehending the past as something salient, Lizzie remarks,

"Life," I say, "is nonlinear, Mother."
"Depends on how you look at it. You may see it as a circle. But it always
    seems like a line to me." She puts the chalk down and wipes her fingers
    daintily on a paper towel. "The past is the past."
"Well, I like circles," I say nonchalantly. "The world seems to move in
    cycles, don't you think?" (Perry 1998, 93)

This continues to be a hard concept for Sarah to grasp, but Lizzie knows that Sarah will never get over the pain that her mother/daughter's transmigration has caused her if she does not understand and become a conscious part of the circle. So piece by piece, one link after another, Lizzie uses the quilt to reveal Grace's story to Sarah until Sarah can finally say, "The circle is complete and my daughter sits across from me with the gap finally closed" (Perry 1998, 231).

The quilt allows Grace and Lizzie to return to the past while moving forward at the same time. But unlike Grace, who uses quilting as a way of remembering and recording her transmigration, Lizzie uses quilting as a way of bringing healing to Sarah, who has suffered as a result of Lizzie's and Grace's transmigrations. She wants to remove the pain of Ayo's Middle Passage and enslavement from the women in her family, especially from those who have transmigrated and will transmigrate, (the forever people). In the same way that Maggie in "Everyday Use" would be able to fix quilts or "renew the heritage," Lizzie makes another quilt and "renew[s] the heritage so that it is not fixed in the past." She knows that it is important that the past be preserved, and she also knows that more stories must be told and understood in order for the pain of the forever women to heal.

By so closely linking transmigration to quilts and quilting in this novel, Perry accomplishes several things. She connects the spiritual to the material as complementary elements in this story that could be seen as Ayo's journey to strengthen her "life force" or *magara*, which has been wounded or interrupted by her capture and enslavement. The quilts can thus be seen as a part of "the material," which strengthens "the spiritual." Perry also uses the giving and receiving of quilts to connect "the African family, [which] includes the 'dead,' 'the living,' and the 'yet unborn'" (Ani 1980, 7); she even provides a literal "thread" to connect generations with the small piece of blue cloth, which travels from Ayo's mother in Africa to the quilt representing Grace's life that Lizzie and Sarah make together. And in stressing the communal nature of quilting, Perry includes more recent generations in the circle as she portrays various women in Lizzie's family quilting together.

REFERENCES

Ani, Marimba (formerly Dona Richards). 1980. *Let the Circle Be Unbroken: The Implications of African Spirituality in the Diaspora.* Trenton, NJ: The Red Sea Press.

Butler, Octavia. 1988. *Kindred.* Boston: Beacon Press.

Cash, Floris Barnett. 1995. "Kinship and Quilting: An Examination of an African-American Tradition." *The Journal of Negro History* 80, no. 1 (Winter 1995): 30–41.

Christian, Barbara T. 1994. "Alice Walker: The Black Woman Artist as Wayward." *Women Writers Text and Contexts: "Everyday Use."* Ed. Barbara T. Christian. New Brunswick NJ: Rutgers University Press: 123–147.

Dash, Julie. 1992. *Daughters of the Dust: The Making of an African American Woman's Film.* New York: The New Press.

Jahn, Janheinz. (1961) 1990. *Muntu: African Culture and the Western World.* Trans. Marjorie Green. Reprint. New York: Grove Weidenfeld. New York, Grove.

Long, Lisa A. 2002. "A Relative Pain: The Rape of History in Octavia Butler's *Kindred* and Phyllis Alesia Perry's *Stigmata*." *College English* 64, no. 4 (March): 473–483.

Mason, John. 1992. *Orin Orisha: Songs for Selected Heads.* Brooklyn, NY: Yoruba Theological Archministry.

Mbiti, John S. 1990. *African Religions and Philosophy.* Oxford: Heinemann.

Perry, Phyllis Alesia. 1998. *Stigmata.* New York: Hyperion.

Richards, Dona. 1993. "The Implications of African-American Spirituality." *African Culture: The Rhythms of Unity.* Eds. Molefi Kete Asante and Kariamu Welsh Asante. Trenton, NJ: Africa World Press: 207–231.

Ryan, Judylyn S. 2005. *Spirituality as Ideology in Black Women's Film and Literature.* Charlottesville, VA: University of Virginia Press.

Stuckey, Sterling. 1987. *Slave Culture: Nationalist Theory and the Foundation of Black America.* New York: Oxford University Press.

Thompson, Robert Farris. 1984. *Flash of the Spirit.* New York: Vintage Books.

Tobin, Jacqueline L., and Raymond G. Dobard. 1999. *Hidden in Plain View: A Secret Story of Quilts and the Underground Railroad.* New York: Anchor.

Toni Morrison. 1987. Profile of a Writer Series. Dir. Alan Benson. 1987. Videocassette. Home Vision.

Wahlman, Maude Southwell. 2000. "The Hidden Charms of the Deep South." In *Souls Grown Deep: African American Art of the South.* Eds. Paul Arnett and William Arnett, vol. 1. Atlanta: Tinwood Books: 66–105.

———. 2001. *Signs and Symbols: Africa Images in African American Quilts.* Atlanta: Tinwood Books.

Washington, Teresa. 2005. *Our Mothers, Our Powers, Our Texts: Manifestations of Aje in Africana Literature.* Bloomington: Indiana University Press.

Wippler, Migene Gonzalez. 1992. *Powers of the Orishas: Santeria and the Worship of Saints.* New York: Original Publications.

Chapter 10

Yemoja

The Muse of Africana Creativity

Leah Creque-Harris

The presence of an African divine mother is perennial in the myths and storytelling of ancient and contemporary artists of African descent. The literature of the African diaspora is also full of signs, symbols, and metaphors that signal messages from the maternal ancestors of the authors. The visual and performative arts of folklore, dance, and song similarly reflect ancient messages that cannot be expressed in text alone. This African divine mother is perennial in the way that the elements of the earth are always with us, though we seldom take notice or heed. Perhaps the artists of which I speak are unaware that a maternal African deity might be their inspiration because the etymology of muse is Greek which hides and negates African creative energy. Black feminist literary and cultural critics began to see the uncut umbilical cord still connecting the artists of the African diaspora to their quintessential roots of African spirituality. Marjorie Pryse refers to Alice Walker's acknowledgment of authorship as magic in which she serves as a medium (Pryse and Spillers 1985). The research of these scholars has unpacked the cultural products of our leading literary, visual, and performing artists, and the case has been made and proven that the ancient cosmologies, religion, and spirituality of Africa are operative and apparent throughout the African diaspora in our production and consumption of art. The spiritual underpinnings in the works of key authors and artists can be traced back to retentions of the ancient African feminine divine and traditional spiritual practices of native and enslaved women who evoke the deity Yemoja. While these instances are more apparent in the works of women authors/artists, male authors and artists make similar spiritual references, as well, to depict the lives of women of African descent. In this era of renewed interest in African-based cosmology, it is important to catalogue the spiritual presence of Yemoja in the content of the maternal message to identify a distinctive artistic voice and aesthetic that characterizes authors and artists of the diaspora across a variety of genres and literary and artistic movements.

This task is rather daunting because throughout the ages of the Maafa, the Middle Passage, the centuries of enslavement and colonialism, there has occurred distancing and disruptions in African thought and epistemology to such an extent that there are as many variants of deities, dogma, and practices as there are regions of the transatlantic slave trade. The dominant African religious system that is most widely recognized in the Western hemisphere is derived from the Yoruba tradition of Ifa: Santeria and Candomblé. Vodun and its derivatives, which stem from the spiritual practices of Benin, are familiar traditions in the Americas, as well. The pantheons of the African deities are similar but have varying names and associations. Yet, it is generally agreed that in the hierarchy of African religion that the female deity of Yemoja is among the highest source of female energy and the mother of the popular female deities of Osun and Oya. The Christian context in which African religions reside should be noted to include the Virgin Mary and Catholic saints that are syncretized to secretly worship the supreme deity, Yemoja, and the other female deities whose sacred acknowledgement is forbidden. Regardless of the specifics in which African religious systems acknowledge the divine feminine, for the artists of the diaspora, a divine mother by any other name is still the divine mother. It is the work of the artist to call upon her for creative sustenance. This call out to the divine African mother has mostly been subliminal and a habit of the collective unconscious until, more recently, artists have become more aware, self-conscious, and strategic in the incorporation of African mythological elements in their work.

The oppression of African humanity and the suppression of women of African descent left generations, bereft of alternatives, to imagine their African identities in a space of cultural freedom. Without the materiality of pen, paper, reference books, and the pedagogy of African civilization, artists of African descent pieced together through conjuring, or as the title of an important work of Black feminist criticism suggests, "inspiriting" a textual narrative to connect to the source of Africa—as mother Africa, the continent as the genesis of our being (Awkward 1989). Thus, there are cultural references to the continent as Mother Africa without the specific name of a female deity from an African religious system. Other texts contain linguistic patterns, symbolic notes, and behaviors that evoke African cosmology of the feminine divine. For the purposes of this paper, my usage of the terms of texts and storytelling encompass all the arts. Also, all the figurations of a female deity or maternal spirit will be discussed who closely adhere to the attributes and symbolism of Yemoja as the orisa of motherhood, protection, and fertility with associations to the bodies of water and aquatic organisms that sustain life and symbolize the transatlantic crossing of Mother Africa's children to the regions of African Diaspora.

The longing for a connection between a mother and her child is one of the most fundamental of human emotions. It is a connection that cannot be forgotten though time, distance, and space may separate them physically; it cannot separate them spiritually or subconsciously. One will seek out the other. In African Diasporic art, the ancestral mother inspires the artist, her progeny, in a call to creativity. The mothering spirit of Yemoja may summon the artist in dreams of inspiration. The artist's intuitive response seeks to find his divine mother through cultural expression: the construction of a character who is bereft of heritage; the development of a plot of reckoning with African origins; and the rendering of an archetype of a mermaid or water goddess who protects and defends. The basic universal element of water permeates African derived cultural expression as it is essential to sustain human life. Therefore, it is understood that the divine mother and deity would rule and manipulate the element of water as attributed to Yemoja. From conception, the embryo is nurtured in the waters of the amniotic sac. For birth, the water breaks to bring the human being to life. To live, the human, who is 40 percent of water, must imbibe water to sustain life. The element of water is most essential to the artistry of the diaspora for it is the water of the ocean that separates Mother Africa from her far flung descendants across the globe. It is also the water that serves as the burial ground for those who did not survive the Middle Passage; their unburied souls haunt the psyche of sentient artists.

The question of transmission and retentions of African culture has been documented by such social scientists as Melville Herskovits, Sterling Stuckey, and the like. The early female cultural pioneers—Zora Neale Hurston, Katherine Dunham, and Pearl Primus—assiduously studied African retentions as anthropologists and combined their scholarly knowledge with their artistic compositions. The three were interdisciplinary polymaths who contributed to literature, dance and theater with significant collaborations with visual artists and cinematic producers. What is also most significant about these women pioneers is that each personally embraced African religion and philosophy. Hurston and Dunham both spent a significant amount of time in the nation of Haiti. Hurston became a student of Haitian Voodoo and an initiate of New Orleans Hoodoo. Dunham became an initiate of Haitian Vodun and assumed the highest rank as a Houngan priestess. Pearl Primus, the first to travel to the continent of Africa to codify her cultural works, became a devotee of Shango. These literary and cultural foremothers provided inspiration and insight into the divine feminine that are encoded as messages from Yemoja in the creative works of latter twentieth century and twenty-first century artists.

Hurston's most popular work, *Their Eyes Were Watching God* (1937), has copious references to African-derived cosmology. Cheryl Wall (1988) considers the plot structure as ceremonial ground for Hurston's understanding of Vodun. The compelling adventures of the protagonist Janie are imagined as symbolic initiations into the cults of Ezilie or Oya by Daphne Lamothe (1999) and Edward Pavlic (2004). Teresa Washington (2013) defines Janie's initiation to the deity Yemoja. Janie's fictional initiation into the mysteries of African cosmology is complete when she returns home from the epic storm and reflects, "Love is lak de sea. It's uh movin' thing, but still and all, it takes its shape from de shore it meets, and it's different with every shore" (Hurston 1937, 241). Though Janie was referring to romantic love, I will extend the metaphor to maternal love. Yemoja, as we experience her, is like the water she presides over. Yemoja takes her shape from the shore she meets throughout the African diaspora. Yet, her message directs the pen of the author back to the shores of Africa.

Like Hurston, the anthropology of Yemoja is reflected in the choreography of Pearl Primus's "Lifecycle Dances" to transmit the lessons of life through authentic dance ritual learned in Africa. Primus choreographed "The Initiation" (1946) to portray the preparation that society provides to ease the passages in a person's life. Primus herself had undergone initiations and therefore used a composite of various tribal ceremonies to develop choreography to convey the universality of the experience. Also, within this life cycle concept fall the dance, "Fertility" (1950) that Primus choreographed to represent fertility dances for the prosperity of the annual harvest, for the successful birth of its future citizens, and for creativity. These concerns are all the provenance of the divine mother Yemoja.

African religion is dance dependent (Daniel 2005, 4). Hurston, Dunham, and Primus demonstrate the embodiment of the African divine feminine in their scholarship of anthropology, in their careers of creativity, and in their devotion to African religions and practice. Through them we glimpse the presence of the divine feminine who can be traced to Yemoja. In this respect, we revere them as divine literary and dance foremothers who heeded the call to bridge the separation of ocean and the gulf of language, text, and performance. Hurston brought forth the divine feminine in her literary texts, but also in her theatrical productions of African-derived dance ritual in theater. Dunham brought forth the divine feminine throughout most of her repertoire, most notably the dances of Haitian *loa*. Pearl Primus's dance choreography provides us with a glimpse into the authentic movements that represent Yoruban dance ritual and performance. The female divine energy, in which Yemoja is the Queen Mother is inherent in their creative devotions.

Yemoja energy is ever-present in the post-colonial literature of the African women. Flora Nwapa, the pioneer of African feminist literature, introduced the world to the concept of a female deity in her ground-breaking novel *Efuru* (1966). In this novel the divinity Uhamiri is among the Mami Wata spirits who are parallels to many Yoruba water deities. Efuru's life and identity is circumscribed by her initial inability to conceive a child, which she over-comes through divine intervention. However, when that child dies, she does not conceive again and is relegated to scrutiny. Yet, she has become a very wise and successful businesswoman who out-earns her husband, another stigma in that society. Her life changes when she dreams that a fish in the lake asked her to follow it, and when she reached the bottom of the ocean, a beau-tiful woman combing her long black hair invites her in. She then becomes a devotee of Uhamiri, adhering to all the required rituals. The novel ends with the irony of peace and wealth that Efuru gains from worshipping Uhamiri:

> Efuru slept soundly that night. She dreamt of the woman of the lake, her beauty, her long hair, and her riches. She was as old as the lake itself, She was happy, she was wealthy. She was beautiful. She gave women beauty and wealth, but she had no child. She had never experienced the joy of motherhood. Why then did the women worship her? (Nwapa 1966, 221)

Uhamiri appears in two of Nwapa's novels. Uhamiri is more commonly known as the Ibo Mami-Wata throughout the African Diaspora as the complex parallel of Yoruba-derived divinities associated with water and is conflated in literature with many of the water orisa of the Yoruba. Nwapa re-constructs the manifestation of Yemoja as a great mother who protects women giving them wealth and fertility. However, the children of the protagonist do not live, but she gains stature as a wise and successful leader of the marketplace. Through the blessings of her reinvented deity, Nwapa presents a feminist vision of status and respect for women. Jell-Bahlsen explains that "The god-dess is Nwapa's source of inspiration. However, Nwapa also re-constructs the myth of the idealized divine woman and voices her own concerns and ideals of womanhood. In many respects, Nwapa's heroine is an ideal woman, but she also has serious flaws that contradict customary ideals and norms" (33). Nwapa then rejects the traditional role of Yemoja/Uhamiri and endows her reinterpretation with the role of a mother who consoles and protects women from the oppression of hegemonic structures. African women have always found agency in the domestic sphere and in the marketplace.

The exploration of Uhamiri in Nwapa's novels provides evidence of wom-en's agency in the spiritual domain, as well. In *African Literature: Gender Discourse, Religious Values and African Worldview*, Salami-Boukari posits that "The concept of duality is a recurrent theme in the treatment of Nwapa's characters, and the messages of her writing. The living world is intricately intertwined with the spiritual, and subsequently with the gods" (177). This duality of traditional feminine values of motherhood is balanced with power as in her subsequent novel *Never Again* in which the female protagonist uses her spiritual connection to Uhamiri to negotiate the political sphere. For example, the male anger and force of the god of thunder Sango is contrasted with the female calm and cool waters of the senior river goddess Arugbo-Odo Yemoja. In *Women in the Yoruba Religions Sphere*, Oyeronke Olajubu explains, "On this occasion, the king offers sacrifice to the Yemoja goddess for support. Appeal is made in prayers and song to the female principle to regulate the violent posture of the male principle in the religious setting" (2003, 23). The war in *Never Again* ends in the victorious intervention of Uhamiri, "No invader coming by water had ever succeeded in Ugwata. Uhamiri was the people's hope and strength" (Nwapa 1975, 80). This mode of arbitration is embedded in the texts of women writers of the African Diaspora, as well.

More poignantly, as we look at the features of Yemaya and her associations with the sea, ocean, and bodies of water, we come to see her in the character *Beloved* in the book of the same name written by Nobel laureate Toni Morrison. Beloved is believed to be the ghost of the baby murdered by her mother Sethe as protection from a life of slavery. Sethe and her family are haunted by a malevolent spirit believed to be the murdered infant. The haunting ceases when the character Beloved emerges from a body of water fully dressed and mysteriously appears sopping wet on Sethe's doorstep (Morrison 1987, 52). As Beloved emerges from the dark water, two turtles emerge simultaneously to the ground; she witnesses their mating, "A turtle inched along the edge, turned and climbed to dry ground . . . Behind her in the grass, the other one moving quickly, quickly to mount her "(125). The verb to mount is used in Vodun and Santeria religions to indicate possession. The turtle is a symbolic animal fetish of the African-derived religions and folklore that relate to speaking and silence, and naming (Gates 2018, 113). Visual artist and author, Ashley Bryant tells a wonderful folktale from the Caribbean, *Turtle Knows Your Name*, in which a little boy is plagued by his very long Africanized name. His grandmother challenges him to find out her real name, which only the turtle knows. Yemoja is said to have derived her power by knowing Oludumare's real name. In this way, the novel *Beloved* compels us to consider her duality as a spirit whom Sethe wishes to mother in atonement, and a woman of real flesh and bone whose pregnancy symbolizes her mythic maternal identity. This identity is revealed as the image of Yemoja as Beloved is last seen naked by a stream, with fish for hair (Morrison, 267).

Trinidadian author Elizabeth Nunez further complicates the primeval concerns of motherhood in her novels about the struggles and strivings of women in the Caribbean context, who inevitably seek divine intervention from a female divinity. In *When Rocks Dance* the issues of fertility are peculiarly tied to Amerindian and African derived rituals to sustain the life force of two generations of daughters. In *Bruised Hibiscus*, the protagonists seek solace through ritualistic remembrance of the divine mother, as perceived by the Roman Catholic Church, and its mythological constructs of the sacred feminine. The perpetuation of violence against women coincides with the annual Catholic ritual commemoration to Our Lady, the Divine Mother. The fervent worship and supplication of this beneficent female divinity underscores the desperation of these women to believe that she can miraculously protect them, though in this novel, they have evidence otherwise.

However, the Catholic Divine Mother is not their only hope as Nunez offers solutions from their indigenous culture of Obeah in the form of a living earth mother, Mary Christophe. Mary Christophe, who rescues her from a riotous mob, allows Nunez to reconceptualize and "problematize" the intersection of Christian, Obeah, and Amerindian beliefs. Indeed, the name "Mary Christophe" is at once a hybrid of the Virgin Mary and Christ. Mary Christophe's presence in the novel is also symbolic of an African deity. For Nunez this "real" mother is a traditional African woman who is circumscribed neither by the institutional conventions of the church nor by the ritualistic practices of Obeah. Mary Christophe therefore represents Yemoja's spiritual force of protection that can direct Rosa to the realm of her intuition and transcendence.

This hybridized spirituality continues in Nunez's, *Beyond the Limbo Silence* (1998), in which larger political and sociological issues of immigration, civil rights, and Pan-Africanism contextualize the problematics of women who must negotiate such new psychological terrain as a woman's right to choose. Nunez's excavation of submerged codes of Caribbean spirituality is best demonstrated through the mystical/mythical appearance of the Orehu, the Warao goddess of the sea, a dolphin-like creature "with arms that looked like a woman: (Nunez 1998, 8). The protagonist Sarah's reliance on the physical and spiritual advice of her priestess/mentor Courtney allows her to consider abortion from a spiritual perspective. In ritual trance, she dreams of swimming among mermaids and is re-united with her unborn child. When Sarah experiences a mental breakdown, the Orehu appears again to rescue Sarah by returning her spirit to the surface of the sea, the place where they nurture their young. The Orehu has the spiritual powers to rescue or to drown, in accordance with their cosmic determination of the spiritual needs of the swimmer. They even have the power of uniting Caribbean people with their trans-Atlantic history and to give Sarah (in a subsequent ritual) information that solves the mystery regarding the Mississippi burial place of three murdered civil rights workers:

> I rode on the back of the sea cow across the Atlantic, her ocean floor littered with the bones of the dead: Africans who jumped ship; others thrown overboard

when the cargo weighed too much. I rode on the back of the sea cow over cotton fields in Georgia, the winds whispering bloody tales of torture in my ears. Across Alabama, down the Mississippi the sea cow took me, down to that other delta where the water ran red. (285)

We may regard the Orehu, as the archetypal water goddess. In this regard, we can note the submersion into the essential culture and spirituality of the original African ancestors. Wole Soyinka similarly acknowledges, "the vortex of archetypes and kiln of primal images is the ritualized experience of the gods themselves" (Soyinka 1976, 36). Additionally, for Nunez, the Orehu is symbolic of the reality of post-colonial modernity. To have been saved by the sea cow was to drown in the "conflicting voices of conscience and history" (Nunez, *Beyond the Limbo Silence*, 284). The drowning of consciousness represents the submersion into African culture and spirituality in which all disparate "tribes" are united in the diasporic ocean of consciousness.

The African divine feminine is no longer an unknown only acknowledged by black women anthropologists and black feminist authors. The memories of orisas and the Odu of the supreme mother Yemoja remain submerged such that we may not be able to call her name, but the presence of Yemoja resurfaces just as the strange object, a shipwrecked Black Madonna, Our Lady of Chains appears in the bestselling novel, *The Secret Life of Bees* by a white author, Sue Monk Kidd (2002). The story chronicles the acceptance of a motherless white girl into a circle of black female devotees to this image of resistance, who appeared in coastal South Carolina with her arms outstretched and her hands balled into a fist. This image is reminiscent of the story of Ogun's gift of chains to Yemoja to protect her in battle. Though she spoke to the black man who found her and promised protection, his master put her in chains which mysteriously broke. Though her reference is of the Christian Our Lady, this annual ritual, which provided its adherents with strength and comfort, involved the elements of honey and the evocation of bees which is like the rituals of Yemoja's daughter Oshun (107–114).

The continuity of Yemoja is figured in speculative fiction. Ta Nahesi Coates' best-selling novel *The Water Dancer* (2019) situates the energy of the divine feminine through Hiram's quest to uncover the memory of his deceased mother and her mystical connection to the escape of the enslaved of their plantation by dancing in the water all the way to freedom. He possesses her spiritual gift, but cannot use it without connecting to her memory. Hiram discover his gift when he nearly drowns in the same river in which his mother is said to have danced away. This passage reflects the symbolic submersion into the embedded spirituality of folklore that inspired Ta-Nahesi Coates. Hiram recalls the family folklore, very similar to that recalled in Toni Morrison's *Song of Solomon* and Paule Marshall's *Praisesong for the Widow*.

Coates's version connects the present ritual dances of the enslaved with the folklore. "So the chief told his people to walk out into the water, to sing and dance as they walk, that the water-goddess brought 'em here and the water-goddess would take 'em back home . . . when we dance as we do, with the water balanced on our head, we are giving praise to them who danced the waves" (Coates 2019, 524).

Coates' protagonist inherited the gift of liberation through conduction, a supernatural mode of psychic teleportation from his grandmother, who passed it on to his mother. Coates even attributes this gift to Harriet Tubman and connects the imagery of the divine feminine to the resistance, escape, and survival of African Americans. Hiram's greatest feat of conduction is accomplished when he is more deeply able to tap into his memory by clasping his mother's necklace made of shells—a tangible ceremonial object of Yemoja. Coates's text is a testimony to the power of a child's first memory—that of a mother. Though fragmented, the mother's commemoration through ritual with the ancient and ever-present African divine mother, Yemoja, leads generations of disinherited African descendants to personal, spiritual, and physical freedom.

The literary canon of the African Diaspora is the unwitting mimesis of the African oral tradition in which African cosmology is communicated through accessible modes of ritual: riddles, proverbs, storytelling, music, and dance. The African oral tradition is a dialogic exchange of the gods and the ancestors with messages for their earthly counterparts, who, similarly seek their supplication and presence in their lives. While this worship or divine communion may be true of all cultures, it is particularly powerful within the African-derived narrative structure because the spirit could not be totally bound. Therefore, the artistry of African culture was protected in the recesses of cultural memory through folklore. It is fair to suppose that the ancestors and their gods actively call the writers referenced in this essay to evoke the spirit of the divine mother Yemoja to perpetuate her memory in perpetuity. Without contact, these authors from far flung corners of the African Diaspora portray the same images of a powerful goddess who rules the waves of the sea that bore their tortured souls to shores of oppression. She simply appears as mother, grandmother, or aunt whose recall of African-derived folklore sparks the communication with the divine mother Yemaya. She is Great Aunt Cuney in *Praisesong for the Widow* who taught Avey the stories of the Africans of Ibo Landing who magically walked back to Africa rather than be enslaved. She incessantly calls her to maintain the oral tradition through dreams and memories that cannot be easily pushed aside. Similarly, the protagonists seek the divine mother for miracles through all sorts of spiritual contrivances to resolve the trauma in their lives. There is in each story the deep longing for the mother who was taken away or who could not mother. There is the gnawing hunger and aspiration for motherhood and the affirmation of womanhood. There is the petition for unity among women, among families, and among communities. There is Alice Walker's quest *In Search of Our Mother's Gardens* (1983) for the mystery in mothers "whose bodies became shrines . . . and their minds suitable for worship" (232). In Flora Nwapa's works, the goddess of the lake granted fertility, prosperity, and protection from war. In Nunez's works, the metaphysical submersion into the sea with the Orehu—the marine mammals of Yemaya—provided healing. The Ibos walked back in *Praisesong for the Widow*, flew back in *Song of Solomon*, and danced across the waters in *The Water Dancer*. These authors have become devotees of Yemoja and their works have given birth to the characterizations of women who must negotiate the African Diasporic spheres through miracles of ashé.

REFERENCES

Awkward, Michael. 1989. *Inspiritng Influences: Tradition, Revision, and Afro-American Women's Novels*. New York: Columbia University Press.

Bryan, Ashley. 1989. *Turtle Knows Your Name*. New York: Atheneum Publishers.

Daniel, Yvonne. 2005. *Dancing Wisdom: Embodied Knowledge in Haitian Vodou, Cuban Yoruba, and Bahian Candomblé*. Urbana: University of Illinois Press.

Dunham, Katherine. 1947. *Dances of Haiti*. Los Angeles: Center for African-American Studies, 1983.

Gates, Henry Louis, and Maria Tartar, eds. 2018. *The Annotated African American Folktales*. New York: Liveright Publishing Corporation.

Herskovits, Melville J. 1937. "African Gods and Catholic Saints in New World Negro Belief." *American Anthropologist* 39, no. 4: 635–643.

Hurston, Zora N. 1937. *Their Eyes Were Watching God*. New York: Perennial Library, 1990.

Jell-Bahlsen, Sabine. 1995. "The Concept of Mammywater in Flora Nwapa's Novels." *Research in African Literatures* 26, no. 2: 30–41. Accessed March 20, 2020. www.jstor.org/stable/3820269.

Lamothe, Daphne. 1999. "Vodou Imagery, African-American Tradition and Cultural Transformation in Zora Neale Hurston's Their Eyes Were Watching God." *Callaloo* 221: 75–157.

Marshall, Paule. 1983. *Praisesong for the Widow*. New York: Penguin Books. Print.

Morrison, Toni. 1977. *Song of Solomon*. New York: Vintage International.

———. 1987. *Beloved*. New York: Alfred A. Knopf.

Nunez, Elizabeth. 1986. *When Rocks Dance*. New York: Ballantine Books.

———. 1998. *Beyond the Limbo Silence*. New York: Ballantine Books.

———. 2000. *Bruised Hibiscus*. New York: Ballantine Books.

Nwapa, Flora. 1966. *Efuru*. Long Grove, IL: Waveland Press.

———. 1975. *Never Again*. Enugu, Nigeria: Nwamife Publishers Ltd.

Olajubu, Oyeronke. 2003. *Women in the Yoruba Religious Sphere.* State University of New York Press. ProQuest Ebook Central. https://ebookcentral.proquest.com/l ib/atlunivctr/detail.action?docID=3408550.

Pavlic, Edward M. 2004. "Papa Legba, Ouvrier Barriere Por Moi Passer: Esu in Their Eyes and Zora Neale Hurston's Diasporic Modernism." *African American Review* 38, no. 1: 61–85.

Pryse, Marjorie, and Hortense Spillers, eds. 1985. *Conjuring: Black Women, Fiction and Literary Tradition.* Bloomington: Indiana University Press.

Salami-Boukari, Safoura. 2012. *African Literature: Gender Discourse, Religious Values, and the African Worldview.* Lagos: African Heritage Press. Accessed March 19, 2020. ProQuest Ebook Central.

Southerland, Ellease. 1979. "The Influence of Voodoo on the Fiction of Zora Neale Hurston." *Sturdy Black Bridges.* Eds. Roseann P. Bell, Bettye J. Parker, and Beverly Guy-Sheftall. New York: Anchor Books.

Soyinka, Wole. 1976. *Myth, Literature and the African World.* Cambridge: Cambridge University Press.

Walker, Alice. 1983. *In Search of Our Mother's Gardens.* New York: Harcourt, Brace, Jovanavich.

Wall, Cheryl. 1989. "Mules and Men and Women: Zora Neale Hurston's Strategies of Narration and Visions of Female Empowerment." *Black American Literature Forum* 23, no. 4: 661–680.

Washington, Teresa. 2013. *Yemoja: Gender, Sexuality, and Creativity in the Latina/o and Afro-Atlantic Diaspora.* Eds. Solimar Otero and Toyin Fabola. New York: SUNY Press.

Wilbert, Johannes. 1993. *Mystic Endowment: Religious Ethnography of the Warao Indians.* Cambridge: Harvard University Center for the Study of World Religions.

Index

About the Contributors

LaJuan Simpson-Wilkey, PhD, is Interim Chair of the Department of Social Work and Human Services at Kennesaw State University. A graduate of Fisk University, Dr. Simpson-Wilkey earned her graduate degrees from Louisiana State University. Her research explores African Spirituality, Diversity and Inclusion, and African American Studies. Dr. Simpson-Wilkey is the author of several articles, and she is currently working on a manuscript.

Sheila Smith McKoy, PhD, is Provost and Vice President for Academic Affairs at Holy Names University. A scholar, creative writer, documentary filmmaker, and activist, Smith McKoy is author of *When Whites Riot: Writing, Race, and Violence in American and South African Cultures, The Elizabeth Keckley Reader: Writing Self, Writing Nation (vol. 1), The Elizabeth Keckley Reader: Artistry, Culture, and Commerce* (vol. 2), and co-author of *Teaching Literature and Writing in Prisons* (forthcoming) and *One Windows Light: A Haiku Collection.* Her work has appeared in numerous journals and anthologies including most recently in *All the Songs We Sing: Celebrating 25 Years of the Carolina African American Writers Collective.*

Dr. Eric M. Bridges is a priest of Yemonja and Ifa. He was initiated into the mysteries of Yemonja through the Oyotunji Lineage of Sheldon, South Carolina, and was initiated as an awo of Ifa by the Agbongbon of Osogbo, Nigeria, Ifakayode Faniyi. He is a professor of psychology at Clayton State University in Morrow, Georgia.

Grace Sintim Adasi is a Research Fellow at the Institute of African Studies, University of Ghana. She holds a PhD in the Study of Religions. Her research interests are Indigenous Religions, Mission Christianity, Spirituality, and Gender.

Khalilah Ali, PhD, is Assistant Professor in the Department of Education at Spelman College in Atlanta, Georgia. Dr. Ali received her doctorate in Educational Studies with a focus on Literacy, Pedagogy, and Culture from Emory University, master's in Middle and Secondary English Instruction, and bachelor's in literature and African American Studies from Georgia State University. A former high school teacher, Dr. Ali examines the intersections of identity, literacy, hip/hop, and Black feminisms.

Dr. Leah Creque-Harris is Professor of English and the Director of the Morehouse College Honors Program. Dr. Creque-Harris's teaching and research interests focus on the literature and culture of the African diaspora, particularly African American and Caribbean traditions. Her writing has been anthologized in many scholarly journals and publications. Dr. Creque is a graduate of Wellesley College, with an MBA from Clark Atlanta University and a PhD from Emory University.

Dr. S. Virginia Gonsalves-Domond is Full Professor of Social/Personality Psychology and Former Convener of African American Studies at Ramapo College. Dr. Gonsalves-Domond has provided direct interventions to special needs children and their families and has successfully authored Head Start Grants totaling over $ 7.5 million. She has been the recipient of numerous awards and was selected by her peers for the prestigious Henry Bischoff Excellence in Teaching Award in 2001 at Ramapo College. Dr. Gonsalves-Domond is a published author, trainer/facilitator/workshop-leader, and poet.

Tarell Kyles is an educator for African-centered school Kilombo Academic and Cultural Institute. He is also a published author, poet, recording artist, and doctoral student currently developing his dissertation project, Shadow Alchemy; a decolonial, community depth psychological framework for understanding and completing the transformative processes of the African psyche, in the United States and ultimately the diaspora. He serves as an adjunct professor of Africana Studies and Psychology at Georgia State University as well as the coordinator for the Truth Telling Collective, http://truthtellin gcollective.org/, a collection of activists, educators, and organizers working together with organizations and communities to actualize non-violent change.

Dr. Michael Lindsay is Assistant Professor of English and African American Studies in the departments of English and Interdisciplinary Studies at Clayton State University. He graduated with a BA in English and an MA in English and

African American Literature from North Carolina Agricultural and Technical State University and a PhD in English from Morgan State University. His research interests include African American Literature, religion, liberation theology, and race. He has published essays in the *Journal of Black Studies*, *PsyArt Journal*, and others, presented at various conferences, and is currently working on his manuscript on religion and the Black experience in America, titled, "Real God Require Blood: The Religious Significance of Death" in James Baldwin's *Go Tell It on the Mountain* and *If Beale Street Could Talk*.

Iya Osundamisi Ogungbemi Ifafunmike is a secondary school educator and West African Orisa traditional practitioner currently residing in Atlanta, Georgia. During her tenure as a priestess, she has acquired an array of knowledge surrounding the studies and worship of Orisa practice in various traditions. Currently, Iya Osundamisi is initiated into six West African Orisa priest hoods including Osun, Ifa, Ogun, Egbe, Obatala, and Esu.

Ifakayode Faniyi Olayiwola is the chief Ifá priest of Osogbo, Osun State, Nigeria. He lectures extensively on the topic of Ifá globally. He comes from a long lineage of Ifá priests and is godfather to many who practice orisa worship worldwide.

Griselda D. Thomas is Professor of English and Interdisciplinary Studies and Coordinator of the African and African Diaspora Studies Program at Kennesaw State University. She currently teaches courses in African American literature and culture, Black feminist studies, and African and African Diaspora studies. Her research and publications explore politics and the Black female body, spirituality in the fiction of contemporary Black women writers, cultural and influences in the Black community, and online pedagogy. In 2018, she was the recipient of the Interdisciplinary Studies Department's Outstanding Diversity Advocate Award, the College of Humanities Social Sciences Outstanding Diversity Advocate Award, Presidential Commission on Racial and Ethnic Diversity R.O.H. Social Justice Award, and the Kennesaw State University Diversity Advocate Award.

www.ingramcontent.com/pod-product-compliance
Lightning Source LLC
Chambersburg PA
CBHW022323280326
41932CB00010B/1208